CREATING
A
CONCIERGE

CREATING
A
CONCIERGE

REN FRENCH

PRINCIPIA
MEDIA

Principia Media, LLC
678 Front Avenue NW
Suite 256
Grand Rapids MI 49504
(www.principiamedia.com)

ISBN 978-1-61485-328-2

24 23 22 21 20 19   7 6 5 4 3 2 1

Printed in the United States of America

Edited by Patti Waldygo, Desert Sage Editorial Services
Cover design and interior layout by Frank Gutbrod
Cover illustration by Ren French, *A Play on Views*
Author photo courtesy of Aubrey Brummett, Third Eye Photography

*Dedicated in loving memory
to Elizabeth "Lizzy" Valerio.
You will always be our muse, our light,
our friend. We miss you.*

*Death is but a doorway
that we all must walk through.
Don't be sad for those who have left.
Be happy for the love they left in the room.*

—Ren French and Joshua Carpenter

TABLE OF CONTENTS

DoodleMaBob by Gustave N. von Bodungen, *Tree of Life*

PROLOGUE-ISH

Hello, wonderful people! I wrote this book to help you feel love, laughter, and warmth in your soul from reading something so relatable to your everyday life. Judge me if you want, but don't judge yourself. Laugh at my stories, even if society tells you it's inappropriate. I'm the one writing the story. All you need to do is cringe or laugh. I'll be happy with either response. I don't have much to give this world, but I do have humor, a killer smile, and one hell of an ass. Enjoy.

You'll find many rich stories that set the stage with heavy details and long-winded explanations and some that don't. I considered condensing some of the longer stories, but then I wouldn't be true to my version. The devil is in the details, and I find the wickedest of devils in rich exposition. There are a few short stories created simply to make you giggle and some you may not like or agree with. I hope you enjoy them all. With that said, let's go through my version of a prologue.

Warning! In the following paragraphs, I do my best to explain why you should or should not read this book. If you choose to continue past that, you've been warned.

If you want to read about me and what happened in my life that created a concierge, continue forward. If you don't care about me, then skip to Chapter Two for commonly asked dumb guest questions. I started with a list of fifty and narrowed them down to my favorite twenty-one.

You can also skip to Chapter Three and choose from the list of conversations from the concierge desk. I love books, but I get bored page to page. Consider yourself at a racetrack and pick the name of the horse or, in this case, the story that jumps out at you. However, I do hope you read every page in the book. Each page has a new adventure, a new story, and new characters that come alive to entertain you.

I have a twisted imagination. If you want to rant about anything, then come sit next to me on the proverbial park bench in the hood. I can make a story out of anything, just like my dad. He's the best storyteller in history, and I'll punch you in your ugly neck if you say otherwise. I've written crazy full-length radio plays, short stories, one-acts, and spoof commercials. I've worked with actors, sketch artists, female impersonators, improvisation groups, jugglers, storytellers, mimes, and burlesque performers. An extra-special shout-out to Picolla Tushy and the Bluestockings burlesque troupe. The struggles, tough decisions, and fierce determination of this troupe are to be admired. Everyone I've worked with is top notch. They've all helped create the vivid world of the Rensverse.

I make fun of everyone equally. There are stories about kind people, horrible people, fascinating people, and more. The titles will help lead you to the people you want to meet. There are vivid descriptions to put you in the time and place, as a stage play would. Hello! I'm primarily a playwright, so, of course, this book will be set up very similar to a play. There are stories that have an overall theme and some that have no real point. There are stories that will touch on sensitive issues and others that are just for fun. I like stories that are relatable to my life. A few of the conversations are real doozies, but they did happen. Hang in there. You'll understand what I mean the more you read.

I'm going to explain what some concierges really want to say to you, as opposed to what we actually say to you. I'll also attempt to describe what I'm thinking while I'm talking to you. Let's call it an intimate look inside my crazy brain. Why do concierges look at you like you're a complete idiot when you ask a dumb question? Well, wonder no more. I'll do my best to cover twenty-one of those questions.

Have you ever left a nasty comment about a hotel or one of its employees? Well, guess what, my friend? We read all those comments you send us. We read every one of them in detail, and yes, we laugh at you. We laugh at you a lot. We also smile, get upset, feel proud, cry, and learn from our mistakes. We strive to make our work environment better for your return stay. We look forward to the cool people who visit us time and time again, and we know when you're full of shit. Just because you get what you want doesn't mean we want to give it to you. We don't want to hear you bitch and moan, so take the free breakfast and move along to your next miserable mistake in life.

Being an asshole to us just makes you look like an asshole. That sounds mean, but it's true. We know when you're bitching because you only want a reduced rate or something for free. We know when you're lying about your emotional support pet that's the size of a baby turd or as large as your dump-truck ass. Yes, we know that your birthday or anniversary doesn't come around a farting dozen times a year. Do you really need that free $3 bottle of champagne and those chocolate-covered strawberries? Guess what? You can have them if it'll shut you up. Remember, you may have won today, but you're going to hell tomorrow. God can see ugly.

I'll answer a lot of those troubling little "problems" you thought you had. I'll try not to make you sound like you're a complete asshole, but you probably were. On the other hand, we're not all angels in the hotel industry. We were probably assholes to you, too. It's not fair to say it's always the guest's fault, but let's get something straight up front: the notion that the customer or the guest is always right is long gone. You're not always right, and businesses don't have to put up with your shit anymore to make you feel like the spoiled brat you are. You can stamp your tiny hooves all you want and then shove a golden pacifier in your ass for all I care. The guest will take advantage of us, threaten us with bad reviews, or call our corporate offices. Call, if it makes your miserable, mundane life that much better. Your bad review will eventually get buried, your negative comments to management will be forgotten, and unless it's something that's genuinely important to our core values, no shit will happen. If you don't like it, then go back to your backwoods Alabama trailer. You've never been farther south than your sister's vagina, and it's overwhelmingly obvious to every employee. Thank you for your consideration.

Contained here are conversations that I've had with real, living, breathing guests. Yes, these are actual conversations that I write down after you leave. I have turned them into full stories. The sign of a storyteller is using 75 percent of the truth and 25 percent embellishment—at least, that's my theory. I can't remember every single word in the conversation, but I do have a great memory. I fully understand that someone will probably recognize one of these stories. Remember, it's my word against yours. The truth is better than anything I can make up.

Good concierges can absorb an enormous amount of information, logging it into their data bank. We're walking, talking data storage units that are here for you. Press a button, wait a tick, and receive an honest answer. Honest concierges will give you their no-bullshit answer, based on the first minute of interaction. They will intuitively know where to send you for tours, dinner, and more. We can build a lifetime of memories for you. Treat us badly, and we'll send you to the bad side of town where the bridge trolls will have their way with you.

In my case, I'll turn you into a character in a play. All the world is a stage, and concierges are but actors in it. I'm on stage eight hours a day. Do you think you're not? You're but puppets for me to create my next storyline. I'm very happy to say that some of those wooden puppets have turned into real-life people I'm friends with today. Shout-out to you, Sarah. I love you. You're family to me. I met Sarah and her mother while they were on vacation. She's been an important part of my world ever since. Concierges are supposed to have a certain degree of separation from their guests, but who's to say where that line is? We're all people traveling down this same road of life, so why not pick up a few passengers along the way?

I'm not a fan of labels. A label is created by those around you, derived from the actions you choose in your life. All those labels don't mean a hill of beans to me because I know who I am. I'm a good person. I may offend you at some point in this book. I'm one part sorry, and one part I don't give a shit. I won't be offended if you throw this book on a dirty floor, take a dump on it, or throw it in the trash. I make fun of everyone equally in a twisted way, and I think that's fair. People make fun of me all the time, and I don't get butt hurt from it.

Please don't be a prude. Appreciate this book for what it is, a funny and sometimes mean look at hotel guests. Storytelling doesn't always have to be where the prince saves the day. It can also be where the prince gets bitch-slapped by the girl next door. This is real life, and not every story has a happy ending, but I do tend to like those best.

I'm Southern nice. That means I only talk about you behind your back. My momma raised me right. Talking behind your back is only proper. I grew up in a city with one stoplight; dirt roads and deer stands were plentiful. It was a mix of loving farmers and a lot of backward-thinking people. I'm not ashamed of having a small-town upbringing; it has its advantages. You can always borrow a cup of sugar from Grandma Rich, there's no traffic, everyone knows one another, and you build a close bond with your family.

Growing up in a small town in the Deep South added to the blueprint of my upbringing. *Hate.* It's an ugly word. I strive to never hate, but I do dislike people and certain challenges we all face. *Hate.* It's ingrained in a civilization that's destined to destroy itself. Spreading hate, no matter your skin color, is still hate. *Love.* It brings out the best in people. *Love.* It conquers all. The difference between love and hate is a very fine line, and we all have both in our souls. My hometown is predominately black, with a lot of hate and love on both sides. It was the training ground for my life now.

I currently live in the Lower Ninth Ward of New Orleans. It's a black community, and I'm white with a dash of Hispanic. Have I been accepted into a middle-income black neighborhood? Not by everyone. I get mean stares; people call me names or go out of their way to make me feel unwelcome. You'll face this in any neighborhood you move to, but not by everyone. I stay in my community for the people who constantly show me respect, kindness, and love. I try to be a good person, help my neighbors, and attempt not to stare back. At times, I'm a chameleon who blends into the tapestry of my surroundings, and other times, I'm the lion leading the charge. Hate and love are at war, but love always wins.

The reason I love New Orleans is simple. Your neighbors, coworkers, and friends become your family. It doesn't matter how you were raised, what area of the city you grew up in, or the stares you get. The choice is ultimately up to you, but in New Orleans, at the end of the day, you'll be loved. My New Orleans family consists of Joshua, Deanna, Sarah, Shawn, Annette, Lily, Aaron, Marlowe, Fynn, Danielle, Jennifer, Sam, Angela, Amber, Stacy, Michelle, Ben, Mara, Frankie, Brett, John, Amanda, Brennan, Drew, Kasey, Valerie, Chuck, Bean, Raylon, Carlesha, Lila, Tremise, Precious, NaTasha, Irma, Albert, Floyd, Kenard, Shelby, Chris, Candy, Kurt, Naomi, and Ebony. They are all races, sexual orientations, and ages, and each one is amazing.

I love to cuss. More important, I love to cuss while I write. No worries, I'm not a dirty potty mouth. But if you don't like colorful words, then don't read this book. It will not be a squeaky clean, gosh all mighty, pinch my cheeks sweet book or a trashy romance novel. I believe a time and a place exist for a great four-letter word. I've always strived to write my plays and stories so that my father could read them without cringing from my vulgarity. You're a grown-ass adult, so deal with it. You'll not find the dreaded F-word. I substituted another F-word for it. After writing this book, I giggled so much that I left the changes for your enjoyment. Yes, I'm a ten-year-old grade-school boy who giggles at the word *fart*.

You may think I'm either crazy or incredibly uneducated. I'm okay with that. I'll admit now that my grammar and understanding of punctuation marks are those of a fifth-grader. In my perfect world, every word would have a comma after it to emphasize a dramatic pause. If you don't like it, suck a big ole bag of dicks. Yep, I said that. Sue me. This is the way my brain works. This is my world as the writer, and I'll write it the way I see it. You can say, "He should have phrased that differently" or "He should have . . ." I could give zero farts about how you perceive the way I talk, write, or cuss, but I do care that you understand the narrative. Just read the damn book and enjoy it. It's not meant to be a masterpiece or the next Pulitzer Prize–winning piece of literature. It's meant to be a silly, fun book to read, one story at a time. You can throw it under your baby's butt for a boost, use it as a drink coaster, or slide it under that wobbly leg of your broke-ass table. A book has many uses, and I want you to get your money's worth. Have fun! Life is too short to take everything so damn seriously.

I write the way I talk. I have many Renisms and my own vocabulary. I do well for myself, despite having little college education. I'm sitting here, hitting buttons and cursing quietly. I'm barely finding my way around this keyboard, but I have a secret. I have very well-educated friends who help me with the important details. I have fully formed patterns of thoughts without the benefit of eight years of college education.

Do I advocate not going to college? No. In fact, one of my biggest regrets is not finishing college. It was not in the cards for me. Life carried me down another path. I'm okay with that. I survived the cold, cruel world of being undereducated. I've created universes on stage, and I think that's farting cool. A lot of what I write is a double entendre, a funny comparison, or an explicitly descriptive narrative. It can be cringe-worthy. You can either move past it or read it twice, as I do. If it makes you feel better, I'll attempt to say please. I'm lying. I won't.

I don't pull punches much. One of my idols is Chelsea Handler. She speaks her mind, is a complete asshole, and doesn't care whether you like her or not. She's also one of the most amazing and fascinating people on television. Chelsea, if you're reading this book, then yes, I love you. You're my hero. We can talk more about this on one of your many talk shows. Who am I kidding? She's the one person I'd probably be too scared to have a conversation with. I would either piss my pants or pass out from sheer nerves.

I may sound bitter and jaded, but I'm far from it. The one thing I don't want this book to be is a hotel revenge book. My rants are truly just me giving you all the backstory. I've changed all names and places and disguised them in such a way that unless you're a private detective, you'll not figure them out. The people I love know I wrote this book. The people I despise will soon know, too. You're welcome. Believe me, I don't want a defamation of character lawsuit knocking at my door. If you figure something out, keep it to yourself. Please don't be the grand marshal of the dingleberry parade. The stage names I've created are simply for your enjoyment. I'm quite proud of them.

I have a sharp tongue and can be extremely quick witted. That's my superhero power. Don't be jealous of it. I've worked for numerous hotels, restaurants, bars, retail stores, charity organizations, and more. After all these jobs, I've earned that superhero power, fair and square. Shout-out to everyone I've worked with because chances are, you're somewhere in these pages. I do want to give a very special shout-out to my friend Margie. You rock my world with your kindness, singing voice, and unwavering support. Thank you. Margie is the best example of building a relationship with a person I met on the street. It took me a long time to build the relationships I have, and they mean everything to me. My friends are like my family. If you screw them over, I'll destroy you. I don't mean in a violent, gut-wrenching, physical harm way. I'll annihilate you with my words. Having a superhero power is awesome. The pen is mightier than the sword, and my pen is deadly.

Finally, I want you to laugh loud and with your whole body. I want you to get nasty, cry so hard that your makeup runs, uncontrollably fart, kick yourself, lose control of your body, and, in general, be a freak. I love to laugh, and, more important, I love to make people laugh. I hope you read this book and escape into another world. Escaping was all I wanted to do as a child, but that's a story for another place and another time. Welcome to the Rensverse.

DoodleMaBob by Joshua Carpenter, *Rensverse*

CHAPTER ONE

JOURNEY TO THE DESK

My name is Ren, and I'm a concierge in the greatest city in the world, New Orleans. I'm not a high-class concierge, the most professional concierge, or even the best concierge in this city, but I am the best at one thing: how to treat you like a person. All I ask is that you give me the same respect and pay it forward. Please feel free to tip me, but it's okay if you don't. I'll still like you. However, don't think I didn't see you tip the bellman $5 for carrying your bag ten feet, and you couldn't tip me for twenty minutes of my time? I'm not bitter, just passive-aggressive, but you'll never know. I haven't always been a concierge, but I love that I've found my way into this profession. I say "found" because it was never my intention to be a concierge. I was very happy being a foul-mouthed bartender, but my life took a different turn.

My hotel is the best place in the world to work. I love my employers, whether this book gets me in trouble with them or not. I have read other books written by concierges or front desk agents that slam their employers. They wrote their books out of pure hatred, spite, or boredom, but I'm just spitballing with that theory.

There is a well-known hospitality book writer who stands out, but I won't mention his name. Let's call this person I'm referring to, for the purposes of this book, Sir Shithead. You sound like a mean little jaded hospitality employee who didn't get his way. You misrepresent everything that we as hospitality professionals stand for. You misled your guests and outright took advantage of them in New Orleans, New York City, or whatever city you stained with your presence. You never cared about what you did for them, just about the all-mighty dollar that you could get out of them. By the way, no one calls dollar bills "dancing ladies" or "salivating singles" or any of the other asinine cute names you gave them. I asked some of the oldest valets and bellmen in New Orleans to check it out. They all laughed when I asked them about your cute names. You also need to make a few friends who are concierges. We're not how you painted us and not the way you assume our world operates. Most concierges in this city truly care about their guests. We want to create memorable experiences of our city for our guests and have those memories last forever. We want our guests to come back repeatedly because hospitality is the backbone of our city. It employs half of New Orleans, and we're very proud that we know what Southern hospitality means. The employees who work as concierges, tour guides, and park rangers and in restaurants, museums, art galleries, and so many other businesses are the gears that run this historical three-hundred-year-old city. Please stay in whatever sad asshole you crawled into.

Whew! I'm glad I got that out of my system. I've wanted to say that since I read that author's book. However, damn it, I do admire Sir Shithead for all the hard work and time he put into writing his book. It is not an easy task. He's one of the reasons I'm writing *this* book. Thank you, Sir Shithead. Thank you for being such a giant prick that I felt the need to write my own book to defend the concierges of the City of New Orleans. I would give you the middle finger, but I'm afraid you'd ram your butt down on it and then expect a twenty-dollar bill for my service. All I would get from it would be a stinky finger, and that wouldn't be very fair to me.

Did I mention that I also go into long tangents when I feel passionate about a subject? I was saying how much I love my employers. I've been with them for ten years, and although my journey through their ranks has not always been perfect, it's been amazing. I won't bore you with all the details, but without some of my backstory, you won't be able to understand my past or won't stick around for the fun stories that follow. Let's start at the beginning.

I attended a tiny public school in North Louisiana. My town is so small that if you farted hard and squinted from the smell, you'd blow right past its only interstate exit. There was only one stoplight downtown and a flashing light by the school when I was a kid. Get the picture yet of how small it was?

I graduated in a senior class of thirty-nine people. It was about as backwoods as you could get, and a quarter of the girls in my class were pregnant. This shouldn't surprise you because small-town kids in my neck of the woods start making babies in the eleventh grade. When you go to school in the middle of nowhere, there's nothing to do but throw a spare tire on the fire, drink, and screw.

It was a predominantly black school, with a few white people mixed in. I had a lot of black "girlfriends," and most of the big black guys liked me, so I always stayed out of trouble. I was bullied more by the white, goat-loving, town asshole than any of the black kids I attended school with. I wouldn't say I was popular, but my brother was, so that afforded me a certain level of comfort. Don't get me wrong—I was still bullied because of my small stature but never to the point that I felt threatened. Sure, I wanted a few people to impale themselves on the sharpened end of a number-two pencil, but what bullied kid wouldn't want that?

This was a time when kids solved their problems with fists, not guns. I got my ass handed to me on a silver platter several times, but guns in school were never an issue. I feel sad for today's generation, growing up in a gun-violent society. It has become the norm in schools, and that's not right. Kids shouldn't be scared to go to school. This goes out to all the bullies in the world—stop! You get one turn at a good life. Stop wasting it by being a pathetic, nasty person. You solve nothing by putting other people down. Stop and think about the outcome of your actions. What you say and do to someone else has lasting effects on that person way past high school. Being bullied is something that you carry with you, and it barricades you from a world that you shouldn't be denied.

I was never scared to go to a mostly black school. I thought it was hell's cool to be a white guy with an old black woman's soul being raised by a white father and a Spanish mother. I was and still am a mutt. I had a few good friends, and the rest could go suck a bag of piping hot dicks. You know who you are.

At our twenty-year high school reunion, I was very clear about who I liked and who I didn't. I want to point out Lady Cheer Bowhead. She always rubbed me the wrong way when she rubbed every guy on the football team the right way. My feelings toward her hadn't changed in twenty years. Lady Cheer Bowhead whored around with my brother in high school and broke his heart. I still look at her with contempt. I know, I should be a better person, and disliking anyone for twenty years only adds time to my sentence in hell. However, I couldn't stop thinking that her hooha must be the size of Carlsbad Caverns. I could drive an entire herd of

Texas Longhorns through and still have room for my Bronco. Lady Cheer Bowhead was still attempting to thrust her jagged claws wrist deep into the back of everyone's neck like a flat-footed cheerleading beast. Grow up, girl, this is not a reshoot of *Mean Girls*, and you don't win an award for being an awful person.

I was never going to get stuck in my hometown. There were not many options of things to do in such a small town. Who will I screw this month? Which gas station employee should I beg beer from tonight? Or how will I get my ass kicked this week? To hell with all that bullshit! I wanted to get the hell out of Dodge and leave that hole of a small, closed-minded, sorry excuse for a city behind me as fast as my feet could take me.

Most of my family still lives there. They've built a great life, but it didn't work for me. I was lucky. My parents didn't want that life for me either. I have amazing, loving parents. They've been together for a hundred years and have always been there for me. My mother is an extremely judgmental but very loving woman. I didn't understand it then, but I understand it now. She was hard on me to drive me out of town. She wanted me to have a better life, one that she couldn't. She was strict, to say the least. My father says it's because she was from another culture and to accept her ways, but I never believed that.

I came along very late in their lives. I always felt that I was more of an extra child than a miracle. Don't get me wrong, my mother and father are not the villains of this story. My parents love me very much, but back then they had a very difficult way of showing it. I first saw my parents kiss in front of me was when I was seventeen, and I nearly fell on the floor. Showing emotions was not typically done in my family. It wasn't until years later when my parents got older that we learned to hug one another. We learned to openly say, "I love you," when leaving the house or hanging up the phone. It was how we were raised, and the emotions were implied. The sad thing is, I picked up a few of those traits and struggle against them today.

I emulated several of my mother's more interesting qualities, but I became more like my father. My heart, my hardworking attitude, my bull-headed stubbornness, my ability to deflect affection, and my creativity came from my father. Before he retired, my father was a nice, caring post office clerk. He was everyone's pop. Sadly, back then he often got taken advantage of by people.

My dad is honest to a fault, but he is not perfect. None of us are. Still, he is the person who taught me to live my own narrative. I should explore, never fear something new, learn a little about everything but not a whole lot about one thing, work smart and not hard, and know that there's "a place for everything and everything in its place." My father is a walking cliché. I don't think I'll ever live my life as well as he has lived his.

My parents are my heroes. Shout-out to Joseph and Maria. Shout-out to my brothers and sisters, too: Johnny, Cindy, Rebecca, and Bobby. The best "damn it kids" on the block. While I'm at it, shout-out to other family members, too! Lots of love to Becky, Toby, Adam, Thomas, Zech, Randy, Brandi, Debbie, Ashlei, and Caden.

I was a late bloomer, late to have sex, late at dating, basically late at everything that everyone else was doing years before me. I was the shortest in my class until senior year. I was late at growing. I had a very obsessive-compulsive personality and needed to touch everything ten times, which often made me late for everything. I was late in having friends. I had one best friend. Her name was

Susan. I was too late in loving her. She died during my senior year of high school. I often wonder how different my life would have been if she'd have lived. I miss her to this day, and her memory still haunts me.

The worst thing in life is to lose your best friend at a young age. I was young enough to handle the heartbreak but old enough to feel the impact of what I had lost. I remember staring at her body in the funeral home and thinking my life couldn't go on without her. I wanted to die. She'd accepted me in every way, which few people did. I cherished Susan for that. I came to realize that living my life to the fullest would be the greatest way to honor her memory, and that's what I did. I stopped being late with everything because I realized my life could end early. To this day, when I hear Madonna's "Get into the Groove," I turn up the radio and dance. I dance for Susan. This was our song, and it always will be.

I didn't have the high school quarterback's masculine model looks. I was a baby-faced farm boy, and I looked sixteen until I was twenty-one. Thank you, genetics, for that cruel gift. People often thought that because of my youthful appearance, they could take advantage of me. They thought wrong. The more I got screwed over by the world around me, the faster I learned not to take shit from people. I learned not to trust people or let them walk on me like a used rug. When you're a nice guy, you're an easy mark. It's sad that society messes you up so much that tough love becomes a learned trait and true love is hard to spot. As an adult, you learn to fight against your own personal demons. You can win, but it's not an easy fight. Eventually, I became the toughest little shit in the world. I got faster, smarter, and wiser and now have the sharpest tongue in the room. I also learned how to love.

I attended college, and no, I didn't like it. I went to a large university in North Louisiana, which now feels like a lifetime ago. I went to college not to learn but to party, sleep with people, and explore a few choice drugs. I slept with friends and discovered myself, as all people do in college.

I found a love for theater and surprisingly realized I was gay. Surprise! I was a theater major. I won't spend a lot of endless time writing about being gay. I'm not going to talk about my newly awakened sexuality. How coming out was the turning point in my adult life. How it developed a deeper sense of purpose, how it helped me evolve internally as a person in a homophobic society during the eighties and the nineties. This book has nothing to do with that. I respect the men and the women who fought and gave their lives for the rights that I fully enjoy today.

I grew up during a time of horrific history. The AIDS scare. We were told not to touch one another and that "it" can be transmitted by something as simple as kissing. I was terrified. Several of my close friends died from unsafe sexual practices before time taught us the truth. I have deep respect for all that has come before me. However, there were times when I didn't feel safe in the gay community, yet at other times, it was the only home for me. I made the best out of my surroundings.

Me being gay has never defined me. I'm Ren and will always be Ren. The truth is, being gay was a surprise to me, too. Experts say that you're born gay, that you've always known, and there is no choice. I didn't feel that way. I remember the exact time and place. I woke up one morning, and it felt right to come out. I never felt pressured by any one person. I've slept with girls, and I've had many girlfriends. I've slept with guys, and I've had many boyfriends. I chose to come out at the time when it was right for me to feel that way. I admire people who have always known at a young age, but it's different for everyone. For me, it was a choice, like everything in my life. I'm okay with that. In life, you learn as you go, and I did.

Theater was the only department where I felt safe to express myself. I could escape and be someone else in any time and place. I could write crazy stories, and people would listen to them. I could explore outlets in my mind that I've always wanted to explore. I could get my ideas out on paper, through acting on stage, by improvisation, or in a dozen other ways, and I loved it. I loved the collaborative efforts made by artists in my profession and even the criticism from my peers with each piece I wrote. Honest, constructive criticism is always welcomed if it leads to a productive outcome. Otherwise, you're just being an asshole. I don't get upset by harsh remarks. Bring it on! You're only making me better and stronger and allowing me to see my words in another way.

I'm a very open-minded person, and I've always had the ability to read people extremely fast. The gift of reading people teaches you to see people how they really are. College interactions with people taught me my first lesson in the harsh, highly competitive world of entertainment. One of those people was the dean of the theater department.

Do you know what negative comments from the dean of an educational institution do to a young mind? They enhance the student, make him view the world in a whole other light, and seriously piss him off. I'll honor that mean witch of a dean whose name I won't type here by calling her Busted Cherry. She had the nerve to tell me that I wasn't creative enough to make it in this business. That I'd never go anywhere in life because I was poor and uneducated. My upbringing didn't warrant her time or energy. She made me feel small and worthless with every glance. She became the comparison or the foundation for every villainous character I would meet in the real world or create on a stage.

If you could only see me now, Busted Cherry. My life is amazing. I pray you're reading this or being told about your part in this book. You were wrong about me. I like to imagine you're sitting somewhere, scratching your dried-up old puss and biting your cracked lips. You're stroking a hairless Chihuahua, alone in a rocking chair, drooling. Out of pure hatred for me, you're probably devising a revenge plan right now. I'm okay with that. I hope you do. It would be the most creative, accredited act to come out of your tenure at that school. If you hadn't been such a miserable person toward me, maybe I'd have something nice to say. You weren't. I don't. Thank you.

Busted Cherry's undeserved hatred for a kid from the sticks is another reason why I wrote this book. It helped drive me to be the best at everything in my life, so that one day I could look back and say, "Fart you," with confidence. Although my father told me not to be scared in life, I was. This knocked the scared right out of me. "Fart you!" I mean that with every fiber of my being, not out of spite but with respect. I have earned this right over a lifetime of struggle. I don't hand out these farting gems lightly because the words we use have weight, and I understand that. However, I hand this gem to you, Busted Cherry—not just from me but from everyone who was ever treated the way you treated me. Shame on you.

There were some very positive experiences in college, too. I loved the overprivileged dick holes whose parents paid for every penny of their college experience. My farm-raised parents couldn't afford my books, but we figured it out. I'm not bitter. I'm not mad that I had to work two minimum-wage jobs just to pay my way through a college experience that I couldn't even finish. No. I'm not bitter at all. There were struggles, and there always will be. I loved the summer college acting gigs I performed in. I gained valuable life experience during summer stock, and my talent grew. It gave me great stories and memories to write about. The summers were my favorite part of college.

I think everyone should go to college, and I by no means want you to think I'm against it. College is what you make of it. I realized too late that it was something I should've been better at. I should have strived to complete college, but I didn't. I have very few regrets in my life, but not finishing college is ranked up there in my top three.

It was years later when Facebook became all the rage that I reached out to someone I attended college with during those interesting times. I thought that maybe he had changed, and we could be friends now that we were both older and more mature. That was a big mistake on my part. It was one of those rare cases where I found someone I knew, who knew someone, who was friends with someone, and blah blah blah. I remember his real name, but let's just call him Dickbag Dave. This human piece of walking trash treated me like a disease. His response to my friendly reminder of our college days was the equivalent of shooting a hot load of lava in my face while laughing. It's okay. He can go fart himself, and I can spill a little tea in a warm-hearted story.

The rumor was, he was allegedly sleeping with Busted Cherry, the evil theater department dean spawned by the devil. She adored him, so it should be no surprise that the two pig poops found each other. He was SAG and her ticket to Broadway or Hollywood. I didn't realize that trying to screw your way from the bottom could make the cream rise to the top. Good luck to both of you with that. Guess what, Dickbag Dave? I heard you made it all the way into one commercial and a failed television show. My guess is that your acting was as stale as that wilted cherry stem you kept trying to tie with your tongue. I hope all those years of being a sloppy rent boy to Busted Cherry were good for you because karma is a bitch. The carpool to hell is crowded, and I hope you enjoy her company.

That covers my fun college life. It had its ups and downs. I made friends, I lost friends, but overall it was the best I could make of it. My life marched on toward the next life-changing moment, bad decision, or passion to discover. Let's jump ahead a few more years.

I was a retail store manager for fourteen years after dropping out of college. I worked for a major movie and music retail company in malls across the country. I'd found the one job that was made for me. New music and movies were released for sale every Tuesday morning. It was like Christmas every week. I was in heaven, and I never wanted it to stop. It was there that I discovered my love for customer service. It didn't happen in a college business class or one of the many other shitty jobs I had endured. It happened in a shopping mall next to a food court where mean girls and frat bros flirted daily. I found my voice speaking with customers and found my strength as a store manager.

The man who hired me was a rock star. His name was Roy, and he believed in this skinny small-town kid to run a business location for a corporate giant. He saw more in me, and I strived hard to make him proud. This was also where I met two of my lifelong friends. Shout-out to Ala and Zala, my A to Z best friends. I developed a sense of customer service and a work ethic that I'm proud of to this day. I was very good at my job. I earned awards, ran amazing stores across the country, and discovered the professional person I wanted to be.

I also realized the type of person I didn't want to become. I was not going to treat my employees like shit, rule with an iron fist, or belittle them to make myself feel better. I was not going to make them feel less than what I knew they could become. I was present. I was always in the moment and on stage, as a good manager should be. I understand that life is more than where you work. I wish more people would realize that. I don't believe in the philosophy of living for work or taking your job home with you. When you walk out your business doors, leave the job behind to enjoy your own life.

I strived to have an active social life after work. It was not easy for a guy who didn't commit to the casual sex scene. I was very lazy when I went out clubbing. I preferred to watch music videos and drink my beer alone, rather than randomly hook up with a piece of stray ass. I didn't have the motivation or the energy for anything more. If I did have a one-night stand, it was fun and casual and didn't upset my routine.

I have trained scores of young people in my time. I'm still friends with many of them today, one of whom works for a very popular mouse. I absolutely love her. It had been a decade since we'd seen each other, but we stayed in touch through social media. I reached out to her on one of my many adventures, and it was the best decision I'd ever made. She was exactly the person I knew she would be. I had hired her at the young age of sixteen for her first job. She remembered more about what I'd done for her than

I did. I helped shape the person she is today. I impacted someone else's life in a positive way. It's the best feeling in the world to know you've made a difference.

I never realized how important my actions were to her. I never got upset when she couldn't grasp a concept. I changed my approach. Her lack of understanding the problem pointed to my failure as a manager. Everyone learns a different way. Working toward the solution is always better than stressing over the problem. I had faith in her because she instilled faith in me. I treated her the way that I wished people had treated me. Shout-out to you, Alyse. You're one of the most loving, caring, smart, fantastic people I've ever known. The people you meet, work with, and interact with do remember you. You do matter. You do have an impact on them. It can be the simplest thing in the world, but it matters. The customers or the guests you interact with do influence your life. Before you realize it, you glean a little piece from them, and they become part of your personality.

Momma Sue is one of those customers. They broke the hash brownie pan when they made her. She loved movies and came in every Tuesday for the new releases, bringing along her lovely twin daughters; Staci and Traci. She was polite and nice, and she remembered my name. There were many times when I felt like a ghost in my own retail store. The public ignores you, even after you say, "Welcome to XYZ store." Momma Sue never made me feel invisible, unworthy, or part of the retail store's visual displays. She made me feel important and loved.

A few years later, Momma Sue found herself in hard times. It was sad for me to watch because I had developed a deep relationship with her family. Yes, you can develop a relationship with a regular customer. I found a bonus family that extended further than my cash register. Her daughters were older and leading their own lives when she lost her husband to cancer. One day I offered to help with her yard work in exchange for conversation, a home-cooked meal, and several of her special homemade brownies that helped with her arthritis.

After some time, I became a member of their family. I became the extra son she'd always wanted. I'd been there through her husband's death, both of her daughters' weddings, the birth of her granddaughter, and her battle with cancer. She was always a mother to me and a beacon of hope that the customers might not always be right, but they could become family. She will always be my favorite bonus mom. She is unfiltered pure love.

It was several years and many cities later when I lost my job. I didn't have a clue what the hell I was going to do next. The retail rat race was all I ever knew, and my self-worth dropped to a record low. Momma Sue picked me up, dusted me off, and told me it was time to move on. She told me to find a new path. She started me toward the path that led me to the concierge desk—but not without a few other interesting stops along the way.

I had been living in Minneapolis when I lost my job. I had made one good friend. Hey, Sara, I'm talking about you. Besides her, there was nothing for me in Minneapolis. I hated living in a frozen tundra. It sucked rotten snowballs. And then . . . boom! The bottom fell out, and I was suddenly unemployed. What was I going to do?

My skinny white ass moved back to the one city I loved, New Orleans. I could be a retail rock god again, right? Wrong! I couldn't find retail work anywhere when I returned. I applied everywhere for anything offered. I got hired for zip. Not shit. Zero. You've got to be farting kidding me! I had been the golden boy of my company. I was hot holy moly guacamole shit. Yet I quickly realized that I was a nobody again. Where was my new path?

I started bartending on Bourbon Street. If you want to measure your strength, then become a dirty bartender on Bourbon Street. It's like you're in a war-torn country, dodging bullets to survive. You're on the front lines for twelve hours a night with no rest in sight. God bless all the bartenders of New Orleans who have chosen to make that profession their career. My heart goes out to all of you.

I got my first job at a scuzzy gay bar from a man in a threadbare baseball hat who looked as old as my dead grandpa. He only hired me because he wanted to fart me. The interview consisted of him asking me if I'd ever been a bartender. Can you guess what happened next? Before I could answer, he stuck his hand down the back of my jeans and tickled my ass crack. He smelled his finger and smiled. I was appalled, but I had no bartending experience. I kept my mouth shut. Thank you, Baby Jesus, for telling me to take a bath the night before. My sweet ass must have smelled like rose petals dipped in praline rum sauce because he hired me on the spot.

It was only a part-time position, but it was work. He told me to shadow the other bartender, and then he limped away. Luckily, I rarely saw him again after the finger incident. The bartender who was training me—and I say that lightly—reeked of cheap whiskey and bad decisions. Coked-out Kevin had enough cocaine caked on the edge of his nose that I could literally see snow falling when he sneezed. It was sad. If I played my cards right, I'd become a full-time bartender before his next bump of blow.

A month later, I was slinging drinks with the best of them. Coked-out Kevin had stopped showing up for his shifts. I don't know what happened to poor Kevin. I hope he entered a rehab facility or found Jesus, but I honestly was more worried about myself at that point. I didn't have the time to care about him. All I cared about was that I kept the money rolling in. I had rent to pay. I sound like an asshole, don't I? When your eighty-pound dog is eating better than you are, it's time to make shit happen.

I was smart about being a bartender. First, the way your night starts as a bartender on Bourbon Street is simple. You work a long ten-hour shift while kissing everyone's ass who's bought a drink. Second, you stay after your shift is over. You're going to drink or snort your tips with people who don't like you or you don't care to know. Finally, you leave with whatever blue-light special trick is still sitting on the tear-stained bar stool you wiped off ten times earlier that night. The trick looks at you with those "Please fart me" eyes, and you try not to vomit in your mouth. I've seen it a million times. I was never that person. When my shift was over, my ass went home. I put money in my savings account and went to sleep. I dreaded my next ten-hour shift, but it was my life now. I had gone from being a big-time multiple retail store manager with dozens of workers to being a bartender at a disgusting gay bar in the French Quarter.

I was an awful bartender. I made terrible drinks. I got people talking, though, and that's all that really mattered. No one had forced me to be an awful bartender. It was a choice I made, and I was learning from my life choices. It's what you do with what you learn that matters. I chose a road where some nights I didn't eat and some were Coyote Ugly nights. The guy has air conditioning in his apartment, and I don't? I'm there. Don't hog the sheets, dude. There was even one night when I stole a pair of Diesel jeans and left behind my ten-year-old thrift store jeans. I had an important function to go to the next day—don't judge me.

The question you're wondering is, why? I wanted to test myself and see what would happen. I wanted to experience that side of life. I wanted to become faster, smarter, quicker, and wiser. It was like college all over again. Will the dean be mean to me? Can I be better than the people around me, or will society dictate my fate? Am I worthless now that I don't matter to other employees? Will I lose the person I worked so hard to become? The answer was no. I didn't lose that person. He'll always be a part of me. I have the stories to prove it. I could have been a bartender for years, and I'd still be the person I am today. Little did I know that being a bartender was exactly what I would be for many, many, many years to come.

I was getting by the best I could. I had jumped around to a few bars at this point. At one bar, I was pushed into a blacked-out back room. Before I knew it, my junk had been fondled by a dozen people. I'd expected this from a gay bar, but this was a college bar. I didn't know who those people were, but did it really matter? It was rude. I hoped my dirty, sweaty, bartender balls smelled good rolling around in their hands. An older bartender once told me not to shower because no one likes dirty balls. The advice worked.

However, I decided to go back to working in the gay bar scene and taking nightly showers. At least, there I would get respect, right? Nope! There was this one time when I was carrying a forty-pound bag of ice up stairs littered with gay men. They refused to move out of my way, which was annoying on its own. I felt a hand creep up my leg, carefully but fast. Next, I felt a giant thumb the size of a thick dart, searching for its target. The degradation of working in any bar is real. I heard a delicate whisper in my ear from my newfound lover, "Do you like that? Because I have something bigger to stick up there." Working in a bar is not a game. You don't get fifty points for piercing the inner bull's-eye.

I threw the bag of ice in Caligula's face, knocking him down the stairs, along with a few other men. They landed with a hard thud in what could only be described as a gay orgy scene. There were moans and groans, and I smiled. I had become Naomi in my all-time favorite movie, *Showgirls*. I'd knocked that old asshole down the stairs and then yelled at him, "No tip, no touch!" I don't know why those words came out of my mouth. I had never said that before in my life. I felt like a prostitute.

I was fired that night, as I should've been. Yes, the douchebag had harassed me first, but that's sadly part of the gig. I should have controlled my temper. I'm better than that. I could have killed that guy, but you don't think of that when you're in the moment. You just react. Why did I keep working at bars? The money was freaking awesome. You could work three days in a nasty bar and make more money than working two weeks in a retail job. I knew that my time in that hell was just a steppingstone to what I was aiming for.

The next bar was very nice. I liked the owners, the guys were hot, the pay was amazing, and there was no dance floor. Unfortunately, there were sweaty male dancers gyrating on top of the bar, stealing my tips. The owner liked to hire dancers with ripped bodies who were as dumb as a box of rocks. They were always "straight" or "gay for pay." I rarely made friends with the dancers. They would knock over my drinks and then act like it was my fault for putting a drink on the bar. Watch where you're shaking your ass, dude. I share this bar with you. Your ass cheeks are filled with my money. You can keep the change, but give me the bills. You do you and let me do me, dude.

I'll acknowledge that dancers work hard for their money, and it's not easy for them to keep their bodies in tip-top shape. Kudos to all of you. The only job with higher turnover than bartending is dancing. Dancers age faster with each dollar bill slipped down their thongs. The eye candy every night was nice, but the job got old quick. I parted ways with it faster than a dancer parts his ass cheeks for a twenty. I said thank you and moved down the street.

The breaking point was not from the gross old gay man, the dancers, fingers in the ass, or one of the many insults hurled at me nightly; it was from a mean girl with a lit cigarette. I was working in a very clean nonsmoking bar at the time, and I noticed a drunk white college girl, smoking. This was the worse type of stupid privileged twat you'd fart with on Bourbon Street. I asked her nicely to put the cigarette out since we were a nonsmoking establishment. That little bloody panty stain lit up a second cigarette right in front of me. She told me to go suck my boyfriend's asshole and tell her how it tasted. Points for creativity.

I grabbed the cigarette out of her mouth, extinguished it on her fake plastic boob, and pushed her toward the door. I could smell flesh searing on her chest. I admittedly had come to work stoned that night, my bad. The details are hazy. What I do remember is that she kicked the living shit out of me. I was sore for weeks. I had bruises in places I didn't know I could bruise. My dick felt like someone had been playing tug-of-war with it. Again, a drunk white college girl is the worse type of stupid privileged twat you do not want to fart with on Bourbon Street. Should I repeat that warning again? I think you get the drift.

It was at this point that my time as a bartender came to an end. I was fired from that job. A few weeks later, I packed up all my earthly belongings and headed out of New Orleans. It's not you, it's me. I love you, girl, but I gotta go.

I moved to New York City to live with a "special friend" and didn't even know his middle name. We liked each other, but it wasn't serious yet. It sounds crazy to move halfway across the country with nothing to my name, but I never do anything half-assed. I decided to take a chance on life. Either I would fall in love, or I'd just made a huge mistake. He was my ticket out of town, and I was jumping on board. Sorority girl hulk was the catalyst, and running a thousand miles away to New York City was the answer.

It was time for an adventure. I'd been squirreling money away for a reason, and this was it. The Big Apple. The place where Broadway ruled supreme, dreams came true, and stars were born. It was also the place where you needed a master's degree to get a server job. I couldn't pass gas in my tiny apartment without feeling claustrophobic. How did people live comfortably there? It cost the same to rent an entire house in New Orleans as it did to rent a closet in New York City.

I moved with a small trunk of clothes to my name and didn't know a single person there. It wasn't perfect, but it was better than being that small-town boy who played in pecan trees and mud creeks. I was there for a purpose. I immediately enrolled in improvisation and storytelling classes. I wanted to be a writer. I was going to learn how to think faster and find my own unique writing style. I was going to get my thoughts on stage again and rediscover my love of theater. I had a thousand voices in my head, and I wanted to share them all with the world. I didn't know how, but I learned. I knew how to be funny, cuss, and make people laugh, but I didn't understand how to bring that all together to form a storyline. I wanted to create a universe for my voices to play in. What better place to learn than from the best people in New York City? Shout-out to Adam. Dude, you taught me how to tell a story like a bad-ass baller. If it wasn't for you, *The Clifton Monroe Chronicles* might never have been created.

I don't want you to think my time in New York City was a cakewalk. The guy I lived with was a prick. I'll refer to him as Thimbledick. I struggled to pay my half of the rent and all the groceries. It was not easy. I had a few lovely jobs and a few not so great ones. The most memorable was working for a horrible corporate artsy-fartsy art store that treated their employees like dirt. They wanted me to treat the employees the same way. I refused. Those motherfarters were everything I never wanted to be as a retail store manager. I fought against writing up associates every time they dropped a damn art pencil on the floor. I did not agree with the way the associates were talked down to by Queen Lard Ass with ten chins. We did not see eye to eye on most employee discipline issues.

I wanted to develop and foster a loving working environment, like that in the city I had come from. I'm not talking about the dirty New Orleans bar scene but the New Orleans culture that made you feel loved. I never found New Yorkers cold or mean; they just don't have time for your nice Southern shit. They don't have time to be pleasant because they're trying to catch the A train express. I'm used to some degree of people being fake, but Queen Lard Ass was a master at it. She was nice to your face, while at the same time stabbing you in the chest. I was a few months into my job when I was diagnosed with cancer. It was stage one and easily curable, so let's move on with the story. This is not a story of surviving cancer. It's a story about becoming a concierge. Shout-out to Queen Lard Ass because working there quickly turned my sweet Southern ass New York City hard.

Through all my emotional turmoil, I never forgot who I was. One day I finally had enough and snapped. Meaning, I mentally snapped, but I probably physically snapped my fingers, too. Maybe it was the cancer talking, or maybe I was just sick of the environment. My smart-ass, sweet Southern mouth went on autopilot. I threw my work keys down in a huff. I told that place to go suck a big bag of pastel donkey dicks. I was free. It was the first time I'd walked out on a job. It felt great! I didn't get fired. I stuck to my principles and walked out.

I learned later that Queen Lard Ass was demoted because of her shitty attitude. I hope they made her clean the basement. Is it awful that I smiled and was genuinely happy that the fates had taken care of her? Meh. Fart her! Bright side of the story, I did make a couple of good friends while working there. Shout-out to Kimberly and Alice, the two best karaoke partners a man can have in New York City.

Thimbledick was not happy and gave me nothing but grief about quitting. I had faith it would work out, and it did. I didn't need his help with anything. I was handling my medical problems and my job situation on my own like a grown-ass man should. You can't depend on others for your own happiness. You need to make it happen and pray someone will fall into your life you'll want to share it with. Thimbledick was not that person. He was too busy playing with his selfish theater pecker to help me. It's okay. I was becoming a master at New York City living. I moved on to working at a lovely yogurt shop with a manager who was better than sliced bread. She was young, and she got it.

There are young people in this world who don't have the common sense that God gave them and some who impress the hell out of you. Christina was the latter. She reminded me of myself as a young retail store manager. She cared about her staff. She cared about me. She understood the importance of treating everyone equally, and I'll always be grateful to her. Shout-out to you, Christina!

I think everyone should live in New York City for at least a year to get a true sense of how big the world is. The city is a playground of wonder. The first snow in Central Park is about the best thing ever. I would sit on a little hillside overlooking Bethesda Fountain and watch people loving life. I would go to Rockefeller Center to see the ice-skating marvels or to the Cloisters and stare out over the Hudson. Life was beautiful.

I didn't have a lot of free time, but I made time to join an adult charity cheerleading organization. It changed my life. I totally earned my gay membership card by being part of the team. I was only with them for one year, but it was the best year of my life in New York City. I found a small, very enthusiastic family. Shout-out to Stephen for always being amazing. He gave zero farts about what people thought of him, even when he wore a dress. You work that outfit! I dare some dickweed to give you shit because I got your back. I love you, and I love the person you've fought to become. Never let them snuff out your light.

I was fierce on the team but not in the right ways. I couldn't dance, tumble, or walk in a straight line. It was not cute. My talent was shaking pom-poms and screaming better than the person standing next to me. Why was I on the team? I have a killer smile, and I was very good at selling shots at bars. We raised money for different organizations, and being a shot boy was not easy. Thank you, bars of New Orleans, for that excellent training! I ran circles around the other cheerleaders.

The secret to selling shots is to irritate the hell out of people until they buy your shitty mat shots. Never let a bar patron enjoy time with his friends until you make that sale. It works. Have you ever tried to get away from a shot girl on Bourbon Street? Those girls are like cougars protecting their young. They'd rather rip your throat out than let you get away without buying at least four shots.

My time with the team taught me how to be fierce, my school was teaching me how to form a universe, and Thimbledick was teaching me how to never live with someone you don't love. It's better to be alone than to be with someone you loathe. The only saving grace was his job. He worked at one of the many Broadway ticket houses. It was my favorite place in New York City. I felt like such a bigwig walking in there and talking to all the creative minds who built Broadway.

Yes, you guessed it. I'm still friends with most of them. Shout-out to Tina. We catch up when she's in New Orleans, and she always makes time for a long conversation, as a good friend should. She's the quirkiest, coolest person in New York City besides her coworker Franny. I met Franny's boobs before I met her and wouldn't have it any other way. Tom and Julian are characters pulled right off the Broadway stage. Their stories are the stuff legends are made of. I love them all, and I loved every minute I spent with them. However, time has a way of catching up to you. The second hand never slows down, no matter how slow you move in life or how hard you attempt to hold on to a special moment. My time had run out. New York City didn't defeat me, but it wasn't home.

I had survived working at an artsy-fartsy, horrible, Suck-a-Bag of dicks art supply store, become a cheerleader, learned how to make yogurt, studied with awesome people, and survived cancer. My cancer didn't slow me down or defeat me. Being gay doesn't define me or limit me. I'm still just Ren. I'm still the person I choose to be, and I love me. When I write a second book, I'll talk more about my adventures in New York City. There are way too many funny stories for this volume. I just looked down, and I'm at 10,000 words. WTF! I'm nowhere close to starting my life as a concierge. I promise to get there; just hang in a little while longer.

I finally broke the news to Thimbledick that I wanted to move back to New Orleans. He started crying, screaming, and throwing stuff around our apartment. Go ahead and break your knock-off Ikea furniture. It's not mine, and it's tacky.

Crying has never bothered me. It just makes me smirk. It's not pretty on most men. I'm an ugly crier, so I don't do it often. I had a female improv coach once tell me that men who cry need to cowboy up and stop being little bitches. I totally agree with that philosophy. Shout-out to you, Yvonne. Funny thing is, I'm dating a man now who cries at a baby wipes commercial. It's okay. You can cry all you want, my hunk-a-hunk-a man. It looks good on you. You're welcome, reader, for that little tease of foreshadowing.

I'd spent the last two years in a frozen wonderland, and it was time I said goodbye. I was ready for the "sweat your balls off" heat and love of New Orleans. I packed what little belongings I had and headed back south. I could already taste the king cake and cheap beer. I was looking forward to my friends, my family, and even the guys who routinely attempted to shove their fingers up my ass. There's nothing like the place where your heart is, and my heart was in New Orleans. That nasty, puke-smelling, food capital of the South was my home, and my heart sang with the thought of being back there.

I was home for a couple of months and landed a few odd jobs to make the rent. I moved into the same apartment I had moved out of two years earlier. Shout-out to Claudia for always keeping the porch light on for me. The house key I had was even the same. Funny how life takes care of you like that. I was not getting trapped into being a Bourbon Street bartender again.

I became a server at the very hotel where I'm now the lead concierge. I served tables for a few years. I became best friends with my hot Latino manager. Surprise! Another lifelong friend. Shout-out to you, Marco. Is having too many friends a bad thing? Absolutely not. I'm lucky in life that way. I feel that it's important to meet people who add to the fabric of your life. I also feel that toxic people in your life should be purged. It's not easy ending a friendship, but it does happen. I don't let negative energy into my life, and as my neighbor Ms. Green says, "Boy, you better take that shit down the street!"

My years as a server allowed me a lot of free time, which was amazingly nice. It gave me the freedom to start exploring the theater scene in New Orleans. I wanted to put all my fancy New York City training to good use. I hadn't endured that shit to come back here and not do anything with it. I auditioned and eventually got cast in a Shit-tastic musical at a small theater. It was by far the most interesting show I've ever been in. I loved it. I can see it becoming a cult classic one day. It was the most off-the-wall musical piece of amazingness, and I was part of the original cast. I love you, Samantha, you keep writing your funky shows, and I'll keep being in them.

This show jump-started my life in the New Orleans theater scene and allowed me to bring five full-length plays to local stages. Yes! I finally got my chicken scratch on stage. *The Clifton Monroe Chronicles* were born. The biggest thrill was not just showcasing my plays on stage but the reaction from the audience. They laughed, they cried, and one lady screamed at the actors because she was that invested in the storyline. I gave birth to the characters of Clifton, Matilda, Miss Sweet Pickle, Bang Bang Tang, Momma Pearl, Chip, and over a dozen others; now it was my job to raise them. I cast multiple actors playing up to thirty voices, and I loved every minute of it. Shout-out to Jake, Leslie, Richard, Angela, Kerry, Ashton, Cammie, Kathryn, Laurie, Harold, and the dozen other actors who gave their time and energy to create my universe. I wish I could give a shout-out to everyone who helped make my dreams come true, but that would be a page-long list.

Why was I not completely in bliss? I missed the rewards of working with the public. I loved being a server in the hotel that supported my theater life. I was happy, but there was something missing. I reluctantly became a bartender at the hotel and still nothing. I moved into being a front desk agent. Fart that shit. I hated it. Working the front desk at a hotel is the roughest, most unrewarding damn job in the hotel industry. It's like the industry has purposely set it up that way to weed out the people who can't make the cut. I hated the whining complaints from guests, the endless being taken advantage of, and the lies guests will tell you just to get their way.

I'm surprised I kept my shit together during my time as a front desk agent. It felt like a ten-year prison sentence. I would rather break rocks on the hottest day of the year or drink battery acid than be a front desk agent again. For the love of all that is holy, the next time you check into a hotel, say thank you to your front desk agent. Even if that agent is a total booger snot to you and doesn't say, "Have a good day," be kind. Chances are, the front desk agent just dealt with a super-size turd that wouldn't flush and hates everyone. Do you want to make front desk agents smile from ear to ear? Tip them. Front desk agents never get tipped. Hell, as a concierge I rarely get tipped, but I'm okay with that. The value of my service doesn't come from a tip; it comes from satisfaction with my job. If that happens to be followed by a $5 bill and a box of cookies, I'll say thank you.

I'm a concierge! A few years ago, my company opened a new property in New Orleans. They wanted a top-notch concierge to run the concierge services desk. Why did they ask me? Did they think I was a top-notch concierge? Had they met me? Did my Momma Sue feed them a hash-filled brownie? There was no way in hell I'd received a glowing reference from any of the bars I'd previously worked for, and I hadn't slept with anybody for the position, but okay. I laughed for an hour before I said yes. I didn't know what the hell a concierge was or what this person did.

Luckily, I was taken under the wing of a very talented, seasoned concierge. She worked for a completely different company, but she wanted me to succeed in my new endeavor. She made me realize that when you're a concierge in New Orleans, you don't represent only your hotel, you represent the city. Thank you to my mentor, Melissa. You rock!

She also taught me a very valuable lesson—fake it until you make it! I faked the shit out of my first year. I did it well, too. I had the confidence of someone who had been a concierge for a hundred years. The only note I got was that my attitude had to change to conform to a more professional position. I'm still working on that part.

I have a bartender attitude. I don't like to bullshit people. I met the hotel halfway and stopped being such an asshole. My smartass mouth had always gotten me into trouble. Now it was time to use it as a superpower for kindness. I started whispering my loathing of humankind into the lobby bush next to me. It doesn't talk back, and it always listens. I also have a network of concierge friends who are the best in the field. Shout-out to Leah, Elijah, Christine, Danny, Alan, Peter, Debbie, Travis, Philip, Ebony, Rob, Anita, Geoff, and Isabelle.

I guess I'm doing something right. I'm still employed here. Little did I know what the hell I was signing up for. Little did I know this would be my next career. Little did I know that I would love being a concierge as much as I love being a writer. I could be a concierge forever, but I do have bigger dreams. I have dreams that my stories will become a television series or an international best-selling book. How awesome would that be! I would invest the profits into opening a small bed-and-breakfast, with weekend entertainment included. The first ever no-bullshit B&B equipped with a full theater for burlesque and storytelling shows. If you don't like your stay here, then get the fart out. I want to be my own boss with my own rules. Be kind or leave.

At the time of writing this sentence, I have now been a lead concierge for five years. It's been a hell of a ride so far. I was thrown on this desk and told to "Make it work, or you won't have a job in a year." Challenge accepted.

My first step was to learn every tour company in the city. The one thing you don't want is to be considered a third-party tour desk. It's a dirty curse word in the concierge world. Tour desks are the bottom feeders of the concierge world. They steal jobs from hotel-employed concierges and don't give a shit about your stay and even less about building your memories. Sorry, but not sorry for being an asshole about this. They're people pretending to be concierges when all they're doing is hocking tours for a tip and a small kickback. It's all about getting that booking, getting that cash in their pocket, and never seeing the guest again. I wish to emphasize that not all tour desk agents will treat you this way, but if you're staying at a hotel that does not have a "hotel-employed concierge services department," then cancel your reservation and stay at a hotel that does. Trust me on this; you will thank me later.

How do concierges stand out from tour desks? They build a relationship with the best tour companies in the city. New Orleans is a well-oiled machine with complex gears. We all work together to succeed. We care about the guests and want to make sure they have an amazing time. Most tour companies in New Orleans are not just good at their jobs but are fan-farting-tastic, employing the best tour guides from every corner of life.

The tour guides of New Orleans know every dirty secret, hidden bar, and dirty street corner; every jazz song created; and every romantic story. They will even make time to hold your hand through history as you cry your eyes out. They can tell you who scratched their butt where, when a tree was planted, and every tombstone of every person buried in Saint Louis Cemetery #1. Shout-out to Angela, Duckie, Dartanya, Luke, Amy, Gwen, Cindi, Michael, Peter, Patrick, Christophe, Goose, Isaac, Jessica, Barbara, Israel, Mario, Kim, Vicki, Teddy, Wanda, Ozzy, Brett, Stella, and the hundred other tour guides in New Orleans.

Take my advice and sign up for a city tour through your hotel-employed concierge services department. Don't be that guest who only wants to get drunk and puke on Bourbon Street. The only highlight of your trip will be praying to God that you'll never get that drunk again. You'll be lying to yourself and God. You'll be drinking hurricanes with that hoochie Bourbon Street shot girl the next night. Experience a tour. Learn our history. New Orleans is a three-hundred-year-old city, and it has a lot to offer.

I'm going to stress this: don't book online! Don't choose a "buy one, get one free" bullshit coupon from a cheap online company or one you found in a roadside coupon book. Talk to your hotel-employed concierge and ask what his or her favorite tours are. We're here to make sure you get the best. Yes, I guarantee if you book cheap online from the Madam Treme cross skull, booty, haunted garden, cemetery, bullshit lady, then you're going to get what you paid for. You'll waste your money and walk away with a head full of fake stories. Again, book with your damn concierge. We have families to support and would love to help make your memories great ones. We took time out of our lives to make your vacation awesome, so tip us.

In case you're wondering, there are also shitty tour companies. We go on dozens of tours a year and not for our own enjoyment. We go on these tours to make sure that you don't go on the shitty ones. We've already suffered through the bad ones, so you get the best ones in the city. I love the tour companies I work with, and I've broken up with the ones that are crawfish crap.

There are a dozen restaurants in any direction you might walk. To say they're plentiful is an understatement. I gained twenty pounds in my first six months working this desk. Damn this job. I suffer eating at all our restaurants just for you! It's okay. My larger, more muscular body proves just how good they are. The food is amazing at nearly every place you eat here, but don't take my word for it. I have help.

How does a concierge know which restaurant to choose? From restaurant representatives. They come around enticing us with their menus. Shout-out to Kayla, Erica, Randee, Jennifer, Brenda, Jesse, Meghan, Hans, Jacob, Jenny, Sarah, Taylor, Molly, and the dozens of other hospitality professionals whom I blame for adding to my waistline. I also want to give a special shout-out to the best damn breakfast spot in New Orleans, Two Chicks Café. They've given me a thousand cups of free coffee and buttered rye bread and welcomed me with open arms into their family. Thank you with my whole heart to Ioana, Lauren, Gabby, Olga, Iulian, Tish, Karla, Naomi, Daisy, Britney, Jackie, Mattie, and Chuck.

How do you find the perfect restaurant? Again, hotel-employed concierges have done all the research for you. We're constantly eating at new restaurants and blacklisting the ones where we get poor food or poor service. I will overlook a mediocre dish if the service is amazing, but poor service will kill any business. Guests don't come here expecting big-city attitudes and drug-induced glassy eyes. They come here for the Southern charm and good food. If you're reading this, and you know you're a shitty server, then do everyone a favor and stop being a shitty server. I'm always shocked by bad service or bad food in a city where it's literally the bread and butter of our industry. I know when a server is not a born-and-raised New Orleanian, and so will the guest. Can you learn? Yes. I have. How? Open your heart, and feel all the love that the city provides.

Concierges also don't want you coming back to their desks to report that you ate fried cow turds rolled in a sweet man sauce lightly sprinkled with pickled veggies. We want you to come back and say, "Oh, my God! I can die happy now." There are an overwhelming number of restaurants, and your hotel concierge has a favorite. I promise, stick a needle in my eye, that your concierge has a favorite. Please, don't be fooled by what you find online. If you see a restaurant offering a 15 percent off coupon, that restaurant is probably the worst tourist trap in the city. Don't be fooled by the lady at the door who's just the sweetest thing you've ever met. That lady is on so much lithium that she won't remember your name even if you drive it into her farting skull and force her to repeat it back to you a thousand times. The French Quarter has some of the best restaurants in the city, but do yourself a favor and get out of downtown one night, too. There's so much more to this city than what you see on the surface. This is New Orleans, and it's easy to be an explorer here. Can you guess who can help you with that? Your hotel-employed concierge can.

An important step to maintaining a great concierge desk consists of endless hours of mind-numbing, bang-my-head-on-my-farting-desk reading. I get so sick of reading that I want to shoot my computer. I want to take this piece-of-shit tech bitch and throw it across the room, but I need it. I research everything.

I can tell you the hours of operation of every museum and the names of a hundred art galleries. I know a lot, but I don't know everything. Reading is my outlet to the world. I can fact-check on a website, in a book, or in a magazine faster than you can think to ask it. I'm ragging on reading, but it really is the key. The best place to get updated information straight from the horse's mouth is *Where Traveler*. Pick it up! It's my bible. Do I sound super smart with all my knowledge of the city? I wouldn't if it weren't for the amazing staff at *Where Traveler*. Shout-out to Stephanie, Ashlea, Doug, and the incomparable Lois. If you see a concierge sitting at his desk, twirling in his seat, or clicking his tongue with boredom, then find a new concierge. The good ones will always have a mobile app open, be burning the keys off a keyboard, have the image of Wikipedia as their start-up screen, or be flipping through a New Orleans tourism book.

You'll not find better art in this world than in New Orleans. I'm not talking about generic acrylic paint on canvas. I'm talking about tin cutouts, paintings on old Creole shotgun house doors, and blue dogs. There is one artist named Samantha who burns her work by hand on old wood without a blueprint. She's one of the best artists in the city. The next time you see a young lady with burn marks on her fingers and a bright happy smile, do yourself a solid and buy a piece from her. My friend Aubrey is the best photographer in the city, and she's in the middle of Jackson Square. Treat yourself to a nice gift, and buy something from one of them. At some point in our near future, that piece of New Orleans street art will be worth millions.

I'm only scratching the surface of my duties. There're a thousand other small details that go into building a great concierge desk; for example, transportation companies, wedding venues, music venues, florists, retail stores, hair stylists, massage therapists, baby sitters, dog walkers, spas, nail salons, shoe repair stores, pharmacies, chefs, or whatever the hell you request. Shout-out to Barbara, Melissa, Lloyd, Kaitlyn, and Kendi.

It really pisses me off when other employees say I don't do anything but sit here and look cute. I wish I could just sit here, shoot the shit with guests, and have fun. My job is hard. A great concierge brings in tons of revenue for his or her hotel, while at the same time providing the guest with a great time. It's why hotels need to keep hotel-employed concierges and why it's ridiculous when they replace us with a third-party vendor. We are not just an amenity for the property but the beating heart of it. Don't cut out your heart. You'll not survive. I need to be a liaison for the hotel and everyone's best friend, whether I want to or not. I want to be your friend, and then there are those times when I want you to slowly back away and run.

As lucky as you are to have me as a resource, I'm lucky to have you as a guest. Please talk to your concierge because without you, the guest, we don't have a job. Don't be scared to ask me a question. I've heard it all. The stupid questions, the funny conversations, the amazing stories, and more. I hope you have a better understanding of who I am, what I do, and where I came from. Now, enough about me. It's time to start talking about you, the guest.

How much I laugh *at* you and how much I laugh *with* you are always up to you. I'm here to poke fun at the guests, and they're the main reasons I wrote this book. Sometimes the guest can be right, but don't expect me to jump on your train. I know which side of the battle line I belong on. I have worked with a few lousy people in the hospitality industry, but most of us are amazing. This book is being written by a hospitality professional, and in my perfect world, hospitality workers can do no wrong. We are the bomb. com, and we know it.

[Mic drops . . . resonating thud heard around the world.]

DoodleMaBob by Ren French and Gustave N. von Bodungen, *Itching Questions*

CHAPTER TWO

TWENTY-ONE DUMB QUESTIONS

I wrote this chapter first because it'll probably be the hardest part of the book to write. It's not because I struggle to find dumb questions, but rather because there are so many of them. I'd drown in an ocean of dumb questions if it weren't for my concierge floaties I wear daily. I don't want you to feel like you've been cheated. They're all dirty gems to be appreciated. I don't want to sound like a broken record, but I'll repeat myself many times. Get used to it.

The following questions are only a taste of what concierges might be asked. The questions can be funny, outlandish, and brutally honest. I take full responsibility for them. I hope you find it in your heart to laugh. These are actual questions that I've been asked. I know you'll probably wonder if any of them are complete fiction. I wish that were the case.

Most people don't think before they speak. It makes my job interesting. I don't know what it is about my face that makes people comfortable enough to ask or tell me anything. People spill national secrets to me without blinking an eye. I don't know if it's my smile, my bartender personality, or the fact that I don't look threatening. People ask me some of the craziest shit and tell me stories that equally delight and burn my ears. My mind races with answers, but sadly I can't say them out loud to your face. In the confines of these pages, now I can. I don't speak for every concierge, but I'm sure that most have had these same thoughts.

My crack team of test readers said I sounded mean with my answers. It was not my intention to be mean, but if I don't break it down for you, the point of the answer would be lost. The title of this chapter is, "Twenty-One Dumb Questions," not "Twenty-One Nice Questions." My only request is that you dig deep into your soul and ask yourself, *Have I been a dumbass? Have I thrown common sense out the window? Have I been a spoiled twit?* Have you? Enjoy!

QUESTION #1: Where is Mardi Gras?

ANSWER I GAVE YOU: Mardi Gras is all around us. It's a joyful time of the year when we all come together to have fun, drink, enjoy catching beads, eat tons of crawfish, and build memories with our friends and family.

ANSWER I WANTED TO GIVE YOU: What the fart? Look outside your hotel window and figure it out. You'll find beads in the trees, puke in the street, and the smell of love in the air. When was the last time you walked down a street and saw thousands of bouncy balls littering every inch of the road? You can pick up enough for an art installation. Take your butt outside and walk in any direction. I guarantee you'll run into something that represents Mardi Gras. You'll find your way, I promise. You will not miss Mardi Gras.

QUESTION #2: Do I need to pay for Mardi Gras?

ANSWER I GAVE YOU: No, sir or ma'am. There's no charge for Mardi Gras. You can stand on the street and enjoy all the festivities from sun up to sun down and all night long. You'll need to buy tickets to go to special events, but Mardi Gras is free and fun for all.

ANSWER I WANTED TO GIVE YOU: It's a festival happening all over the city. The only free thing you can do is stand on the parade route and try not to get severely bruised by beads flying at your head. They'll fly at speeds that will cause brain damage. My advice is to keep your head up and your eyes open. Yes, you'll need lots of money for those over-priced drinks. Your gang of drunken white girls in skintight skirts and shirtless frat bros will be fine, but please bring bail money, just in case. There's a good chance that at some point, you'll do something so dull-witted that our lovely police force will throw your drunk ass in jail. I'm sorry. You will need money for food. No, food is not free here. We're a generous city, but we aren't feeding your gang of merry idiots. Think again before you crash our tents and grab a dog off our grills when we're not looking. You'll get slapped for entering a forbidden zone if you're not invited in. Crawfish is not cheap, and I don't share unless I like you. The restaurants are here to make money, not hand out food. Don't walk up and ask for something without cash in hand. The quickest way to get served is to have cash ready and know what you want. We're busy, and we don't like to wait. Please don't dig under a dirty tit to pull out a sweaty wad of one-dollar bills. It's nasty. We also don't want that dirty change from under your nut sack. I'm not joking; this has happened. However, most people will happily give you bread, crackers, and water if you're totally wasted. We're Southern nice like that. You'll need money for incidentals at your hotel. This is a per night fee of usually fifty dollars or more. I find it really irritating when people say, "I didn't know I would have to pay for that." Of course, you do! This is not the roadside hooker shack. This is an upscale hotel, and if you fart up our shit, you're going to pay for it out of the money you put up front. Also, don't think that if you give us cash up front, we aren't going to check the room for damages before we give it back to you. We know that trick, and you're not being smart by trying to pull this con on us. Yes, you'll need to bring a credit card that is not over its limit when you arrive. It surprises me time and time again when people bring no money with them on a family vacation. Do you expect a hotel to say, "Thank you for coming to New Orleans for your once-in-a-lifetime vacation," and then give you everything for free? Bitch, you brought your ass here. Now pay for your stay, or don't go on vacation. Yes, those high-priced prostitutes are high priced for a reason; they're not included in your room rate. The question was, do I need to pay for Mardi Gras? The short answer is yes, you'll pay for everything. This is not a cheap city at any time you visit. You want to have a great time during your stay, right? Bring money. There's nothing wrong with having a pocket full of singles to give out to the people around you. Everything here has a price. It's better that you know that now, or I'll look at you crazy later. And if you were wondering, no, I can't give everyone free tickets, tours, or hook-ups. We save those little happies for ourselves and the rare, cool guests we fall in love with. I may not have a lot of pull, but I have friends in high places. When I do hook someone up, it's going to be someone who treated me with respect and didn't make me feel like a piece of street garbage.

QUESTION #3: How do I get beads? I want the best ones, the biggest ones, the really hard-to-get ones. Tell me all the secrets.

ANSWER I GAVE YOU: Just stand there, wave your hands, and yell, "Throw me something, mister!" Everyone will get great beads. The hard-to-get beads are not that hard to get if you have a big smile and scream loud. Have fun, and happy Mardi Gras!

ANSWER I WANTED TO GIVE YOU: They're a strand of plastic that you'll kill your firstborn to catch. Did you know that some but not all beads are recycled? That's right. There are businesses that scoop up those priceless beads, separate them, and re-sell them to Mardi Gras Krewes for the next year. It's for a good cause, it keeps them out of our landfills, and it provides jobs, but you're getting dirty beads that have not been cleaned, have been touched by dozens of people, and were probably lying in trash at some point. You're wrapping them around your neck and sticking them in your mouth without a care in the world. You may be taking cute pics, but you're also contracting this week's STD. They aren't so cute now, are they? The biggest beads and the hard-to-get beads are tricky to get from a Krewe member. You better have a smoking-hot smile or be shaking a baby to get those jewels. They're typically thrown out to the men who whip out their big members or ladies who flash their rack. It's sad but true, and that'll never change. You can buy beads, but what fun is that? There are a few tricks that always work. You can wear a construction hard hat and dare people to throw bags of beads at you. There's always that asshole on a float who will throw beads as hard as his overly pumped, steroid-injected arms can muster. That shit will hurt, but your construction hard hat will save the day, and you'll get a bag of beads. You can cheat and hold up a puppy. It's just so cute, and people can't resist it.

You'll be showered in beads, bracelets, toys, and candy of all types. If you're lucky, you'll get an expired marshmallow pie. The ultimate cheat is to make a sign that says, "I'm from . . . (insert the city you're from)." People on Krewes love to pour on the beads to show their love for New Orleans. You'll be covered in beads in no time. There is no shame in begging for beads. Everyone does it, and most people love to share. The last tip is to wash your hands. For the love of God, wash your hands. They'll be covered in black grossness that looks like tar. Do you want to eat a fried oyster po-boy with those nasty fingers? I think not. And for both our sakes, don't shake my hand after you're at a parade. I religiously carry disinfectant wipes with me everywhere. Yes, I'll share.

QUESTION #4: Do you have toilet paper I can have?

ANSWER I GAVE YOU: I would not advise urinating in public. The New Orleans police officers will arrest you for public indecency. Yes, that is a thing here, even during Mardi Gras. I can get you a roll of toilet paper, but again I wouldn't try squatting in public.

ANSWER I WANTED TO GIVE YOU: Honestly, the New Orleans police will probably not care where you pee, but I can't tell you that. Here starts the rant. Why the hell do you want to piss on our streets? No one, and I repeat, no one cares to smell your piss. It's nasty, and you should be ashamed to even ask me that. The least you can do is duck behind a dumpster and pee. That's the only place the smell of your urine will be accepted. The worse kind of Mardi Gras tourist is the "pee everywhere on everything" tourist. You're not in our city to mark your territory. Please don't come in my yard and pee on my tree, and I better not catch your drunk ass walking down the side of my house to pee behind my air conditioner unit. You'll get shot. Fair warning, that's true for every homeowner here. There are thousand bars that'll let you use their bathrooms for free. This is not New York City. You don't have to buy something to enter; just go in and pee. We prefer that. The toilet paper request has only come up once. I gave the guest a confused and half-disgusted look with a raised eyebrow. Please wipe your butt in a bathroom and not in the middle of the street. We have enough shit to deal with in the city without cow pile–stepping around your excrement. I was oddly interested by this question, and I asked the woman, "What do you need that for, besides the obvious?" I was answered with a crazy look, which was completely valid. She wanted to stuff it in her beer holder. She didn't want her clothes to get wet when the beer started to collect condensation. A roll was easier to carry in her backpack. Plus, just in case a bathroom didn't have toilet paper, she'd have a stash on hand. You're a pro, lady. I tip my hat to you. I like people who think ahead. See, I'm not going to totally razz the guests. Sometimes a guest has a valid crazy-sounding question, and the reason is sensible. I jump to assumptions at times, and I admit when I'm way off the mark. Way to go, guest, you won that round. However, next time you may want to open with that, instead of a general request for TP. Gross.

QUESTION #5: Can my family swim in the fountain out front?

ANSWER I GAVE YOU: No. I'm sorry, but our hotel fountains are for decoration only. Guests are not allowed in any of the fountains. Security keeps a close eye on all of them. There are several athletic pools in the area that charge a daily gym fee for use. You can also visit one of many local hotel properties that allow non-guests to use their facilities. There's usually a small fee associated with use of their rooftop pool, bar, or observation deck.

ANSWER I WANTED TO GIVE YOU: In what universe would it be okay for someone to take a redneck dip in a hotel fountain? This is not your personal cement pond. I get it. In your neck of the woods, it's okay to throw your naked babies in the dirty fountain outside the Pig grocery store. However, you're at a luxury hotel in downtown New Orleans, and it's not okay here, Bubba. There's this little stream here called the Mississippi River. I'd be delighted to give directions on how to get there. Everyone is more than welcome to jump in, but I don't advise it. I almost wanted to dare him to jump in the fountain. I'd have enjoyed watching our linebacker security guard tackle him. Bubba already had his swim trunks on, so it wasn't really a question but a fact that he was going to jump in the fountain. I shouldn't have given him the warning about security. Stupid, Ren! What did Bubba think I would say? "Yes, please jump right in! How many towels would you like me to provide for you and your dozen kids?" This was a hard one for me to answer without a smirk on my face. I had to muster every ounce of old acting skills and draw on my vast knowledge of bullshit. Then look at him directly in his smug, serious face and not start laughing. Bubba was too cheap to pay for the pool at the resort property, and that's why he was here. If Bubba had read the booking details about the property, then Bubba would have known there was no pool. I know asking guests to read the fine print equates with asking them to find the Holy Grail, but do us all a favor: Read the fine print. I'm a nice guy. I'll hook up the hose, and you can take turns spraying one another. That was good enough for my redneck family; it's good enough for yours. Sadly, I had to say no again. No, Bubba. Your overdeveloped teenage daughter can't quickly jump in our fountain to snag spare change for the streetcar. That's not how a wishing fountain works, dumbass. You're stealing other people's wishes! If you can't afford the $1.25 streetcar fare, then you shouldn't be in New Orleans on vacation. See previous question about paying for shit in New Orleans.

QUESTION #6: Bro. Do you have aspirin? Condoms? Lube?

ANSWER I GAVE YOU: I'm sorry, sir, but any type of over-the-counter medication is not allowed to be dispensed to hotel guests, due to liability reasons. There's a corner store a few blocks away. They can provide you with condoms and lube of any size and flavor you desire. Have a nice day.

ANSWER I WANTED TO GIVE YOU: I'm not your drug dealer, and that shit is expensive. I'm not going to get blamed or fired for giving you any type of drug. If I give you two aspirins from my stash and you die from an allergic reaction, then that's on me. Do you think my hotel will protect me from that lawsuit? Hell, no, it won't. I'll get kicked out on my ass faster than your grandmother's gums on a holiday stripper. Please don't ask me for medicine. If your head splits open and your brains fall onto my desk, I may consider it. You need condoms? First, one man's junk is not the same size as the man's next to him. I don't carry around large assortments of spare condoms on me. Condoms are not like a glove; one size does not fit all. Bring your own. Oh, wait, you just thought your super-cool and friendly concierge would have them on hand for all your steamy fantasies? Contrary to popular belief, concierges are not walking convenience stores, and we don't keep a ready supply of sexual provisions on hand. How do I know if you need a magnum size or you have a tiny penis? All I can see is the bulge in your pants, not the actual size of your dick. The only time I notice is if it's impressive; otherwise, keep walking. I see a hundred swinging dicks a day, and yours is not that memorable. My advice: double wrap your deli meat. You'll thank me later when the rest of your friends are vacationing at the free clinic. You need lube? Great! How do I know which lube you prefer? You might have an allergy to certain brands. We don't provide lube, and even if we did, I'm not burning your dick off with a hotel-brand lube that we got in bulk from an overseas black-market lube maker. These are all decisions you should make on your own and not ask me for. There are exceptions to the rule. If you give me money with a tip and ask nicely, I'll go buy them for you. I have no problem slapping down lube and condoms at a cash register. I don't even need the brown bag to conceal them. I'll delightfully deliver them to your room and give a big nod to your bunk buddy, as I leave with a smile on my happy face. Yes, I'll be judging. No, I'm not interested in joining you, no matter how hot you are. This is a full-service hotel, but I'm not a full-service concierge. Just say thank you and tip me. I need to get back downstairs and behind my desk to answer the next insane question thrown my way.

QUESTION #7: Where can I buy a hooker? Can you get one for me? Where are all the good hookers in this city?

ANSWER I GAVE YOU: I'm sorry. I can't facilitate that request. I wouldn't recommend meeting any "ladies of the night," as it's illegal and you'll be arrested by our wonderful New Orleans police force. I'm not aware of any "good hookers" or a good section of the city for this activity. I wouldn't recommend going out to purchase that item. However, if you're looking for an award-winning bar for a casual conversation, I'd be delighted to provide you with suggestions. Your New Orleans soul mate may be only a barstool away.

ANSWER I WANTED TO GIVE YOU: You nasty, wrinkled, saggy balls, pervy old man. I'm not Hookers 'R' Us. I don't have a Rolodex of lustful ladies' phone numbers. Ladies are not dressed in their fancy panties and practicing their seduction methods while waiting for the phone to ring. I'm sure there are a few unscrupulous concierges with a secret stash of hookers on speed dial who get a kickback for every sex act, but I'm not one of them. Even if I did, what makes you think I'd serve them up on a plate with a side of fig jam for you? I'm not a pimp. I don't backhand my bitches and demand a side cut. Are the hookers safe? First, let's clarify that it's generally proper to call them sex workers and not hookers. I don't appreciate the disrespectful or tactless tone of your question. They're hard-working women and deserve to be treated like human beings and not pieces of property. Second, I wish I could be there when you walk up to a lady and proposition her. You'll be picking your nuts out of your teeth. Have fun with that. I'm friends with a few sex workers. They're great women, and they know how to protect themselves. However, not all of them are good sex workers. The bad ones are straight out of a gangster movie, bargain bin prostitutes from the wrong side of the street who would rather rob you than sleep with you. What's worse is that you can't report your activities to the police, or you'll get arrested for soliciting a prostitute, and the prostitutes know that. You'll notice I didn't call them sex workers. There are class levels, even within the oldest profession in the world. The levels range from high-class madams to back-alley prostitutes, and some of them are not even ladies, if you get my drift. Where are all the good sex workers? They're not living in Pleasant Hooker Village, where all the magical porn star girls live. Do you really think there is a good area for sex workers, or are you just screwing with me? Do you think they lounge around on silk couches and have feather-pillow fights? They're not squealing with delight, waiting to ride on your greased-up pole. I understand you're old enough to remember when New Orleans had the red-light district of Storyville. It sounded amazing with its brothels, madams, and more, but those days are long gone, buddy. The best I can do is direct you under an interstate bridge. You can shop through the crack whores, and maybe you'll find that shiny diamond in the rough, but I doubt it. There's no good section to send you to. Please, just go to the titty bar like everyone else and whisper into a stripper's ear. If her rent is due, maybe you'll get lucky, or maybe you'll get kicked in the nuts. It's a 50/50 shot. The best thing you can do is sit down at a bar, get off your damn phone, and have an actual conversation with someone. It's called speaking, and it's amazing. You may meet a prostitute, and then you might meet your future wife, but you'll never know until you stop trying to buy someone's attention.

QUESTION #8: Do you think we'll get pregnant?

ANSWER I GAVE YOU: I'm sorry, I can't answer that question. Can you clarify?

ANSWER I WANTED TO GIVE YOU: Please allow me to set up this storyline, so you can better understand the answer. A very lovely young couple approached me. The young lady was cute, nervous, and very excited about her trip to New Orleans. She blurted out this question, and we were all shocked as soon as she said it. I automatically did my doggie side-head tilt with big questioning eyes. She looked mortified and said, "Oh, my God, I can't believe I just said that," after which I said, "I can't believe you just asked me that." Her ridiculously hot husband burst out laughing but didn't say much else. They were on vacation, and they'd been trying to have a child for the past year with no luck. They were beautiful. I'd have made a baby with either of them. They were determined to leave pregnant. I asked, "Why in New Orleans?" The answer was simple: two of their friends got pregnant in New Orleans. There must be something in the water. I saw them now and then and offered suggestions for the day. I was not being intrusive, just a concierge who knew a little too much about their stay. I suggested eating lots of soul food because there was nothing better than a home-cooked meal to make a baby. I sent the couple to Jackson Square for the music and the fortune-tellers. If the fortune-tellers couldn't help, then the music and sounds of New Orleans would. Whatever worked to create that spark of life. I don't know whether they got pregnant, but I hope they did. It's questions like these that make my mind wonder. Did a previous guest tell her that I'm a baby-making fortune-teller? If that was the case, then I'm in the wrong profession. I'm good, but I'm not God. I don't create the actual universe, just the universe in these pages.

QUESTION #9: What are you going to do about the loose brick down the street? I tripped and nearly broke my ankle on it! I demand compensation!

ANSWER I GAVE YOU: Are you okay? Can I get you a Band-Aid? I'll call the city repair line to inform them of that dangerous loose brick. I hope this doesn't dampen your stay in New Orleans. The city works hard every day to ensure that our city sidewalks and streets are safe for everyone who comes to visit. As in any city, construction is common, but an unsafe walkway is everyone's enemy. The brick was not on hotel property, and I can't offer any monetary compensation. Please speak with a member of management about this further if you feel my answer was not sufficient. Enjoy the rest of your stay, and watch your step.

ANSWER I WANTED TO GIVE YOU: You obviously never learned how to walk because you tripped approaching my desk, and it's a straight line from the front door. Are you drunk, or you just don't know how to put one clawed foot in front of the other? Guess what I'm going to do—not a damn thing. Your stupid ass was probably texting a friend and not paying attention to where you were walking. I'm sorry that you're so clumsy that you felt the need to blame the first person you saw in the lobby. I bet you looked real cute when you tripped. I'm sorry that the brick down the street jumped up and said hello. This city is falling apart. It's as old and sinful as Sodom and Gomorrah. What did you expect? There are sinkholes that'll swallow your car. You're pissed off because you tripped on a brick? It was also a brick down the street that has nothing to do with my hotel property. You're a little miffed because it just ruined your entire vacation? Do you realize how pathetic you sound right now? You're worried because people saw how stupid you looked? You should be more worried about that busted-ass 1980s hairstyle you're sporting. Don't waste my time with this stupid shit. You're doing nothing but proving how disgusting and bitchy humanity can be. Here's a tip: look where you're walking. It's a grade school lesson that you obviously skipped. You know that city repair line I called for you? Yeah, I never called it. I guarantee you that brick was loose five years ago, and it's going to be loose five years from now. The city has more to worry about than repairing a loose brick that your dumb ass tripped over. My eighty-year-old mother tripped on a cracked sidewalk and broke her wrist. Did she bitch and complain? Nope! She grabbed another vodka tonic, enjoyed her vacation, and then headed to the hospital for a cast. What a trooper! You're a brick-tripping turd, and your nasty attitude toward me was unnecessary and rude. You want compensation for what? You don't get paid for being uncoordinated. I ain't giving you squat. If you were nicer to me, I might have thrown you a complimentary drink, but you weren't. Suck it. Suck it hard.

QUESTION #10: Your balls are huge! Why?

ANSWER I GAVE YOU: Genetics. Was there anything else I may assist you with today?

ANSWER I WANTED TO GIVE YOU: My balls are huge. Thank you. I wholeheartedly appreciate the compliment. Please, feel free to choke on them. Exactly how long were you sitting in the lobby staring at my big bulge? Did you have a long conversation about it with your group of girlfriends and gay BFF? I noticed you were all sitting there, staring at me. The only thing you didn't do was point. Did your friends dare you to come over and ask about my affliction, or did you draw the short straw? Lady, I'm not sure if you're aware of this, but you're not my type. Your hot gay friend sitting next to you is, though. Please ask him to come talk to me. I'll paint a very vivid picture for him or, better yet, show him. Who doesn't appreciate being told that they have elephant-size balls? I love being talked about by college kids in a public lobby. You've just made my life complete. I can now die knowing that some rando drunk girl thinks my balls are huge. That's all sarcasm if you missed it. She's lucky I'm a nice Southern man. I should have pulled them out and tea-bagged her, then demanded those Mardi Gras beads she choked on last night as payment. Please don't attempt to humiliate your concierge. You'll quickly come to understand that your rude, inappropriate comments rarely shake us. Plus, I was a bartender, and it wouldn't be the first time someone asked me that question. You're welcome.

QUESTION #11: Where can I get spanked or find a spa for a happy ending?

ANSWER I GAVE YOU: There are several gay bars with questionable back rooms. I know spankings do regularly occur. I can direct you to those establishments, if you wish. I don't actively attend them, and there's not an online spanking schedule. As for a happy ending, I don't know of any business that will accommodate that request. I do know of several spa locations that have a wide range of other services. It'll be my pleasure to set up an appointment for you or connect you directly to a spa representative at one of my preferred partners.

ANSWER I WANTED TO GIVE YOU: I'm sure that for the right amount of money, any man or woman at most bars on Bourbon Street will slap you around. People in New Orleans work hard to make an honest living, and slapping you around will be easy money. Touch anyone back, and you'll get your teethed busted out. Yes, I did tell you the correct answer. The gay bars would be your best place. However, what I didn't tell you is that they'll strap you to the wall, and everyone will get a turn. Remember that thumb up the ass I spoke about earlier. Yep! That'll happen. It's a little bit of lagniappe just for people like you. Do you think they're going to let you off the hook that easy? Nope! They'll be exploring your cavity like a spelunker in a crystal do-do berry cave. If you're lucky, their friends will make noticeable red marks on your rosy little cheeks with a thick cedar paddle. Consider it a gift from them to you. I'm sure there are excellent professional spankers in New Orleans, too. I can make a few phone calls, but chances are, they're not any better or worse than those hairy bears with big strong hands that'll make you feel like the little bitch boy you are. You want a happy ending? Great! Why would you ask your concierge this? The spa specialists in New Orleans are amazing, but the one thing they don't like is being asked to work out a wad of your goop. When is it appropriate to ask a stranger this? Never. I may be your concierge, but I'm still a stranger. I understand that there are businesses and people that do this service, but it's not advertised. You can't open the local paper and clip out a "Buy one, get one free" happy ending coupon with every visit. It's certainly not discussed over a desk in a public lobby, and it's not part of any room package deal you can book online. Back up, dude, you're creeping me out a little.

QUESTION #12: Who farted?

ANSWER I GAVE YOU: I'm sorry there's an unpleasant smell in the air. I'll get a can of air freshener right away. You're right. It does smell foul. Let's get this fixed for both of our sakes.

ANSWER I WANTED TO GIVE YOU: You are my hero! I have no problem telling you exactly who farted. I heard the puff, and it was funny as hell. I'll point the culprit out to you, unless it was Grandma. She can't control her flatulence, and that's just too mean for even me to make fun of. There are people who enjoy crop dusting their concierges just to see them squint at the smell. I have a secret weapon. It's a can of orange-scented spray labeled Citrus Orange Blossoms. It's freakin' awesome. I know the name sounds like a ninja fart buster, but it's not. It's used in every hotel lobby around the world, and its smell is unmistakable. Here's the ancient Chinese secret about Ninja Orange Blossom that no hotel wants you to know. It will always smell like shittrus when I'm done spraying. That's right, I said SHITTRUS. I can spray until the cows come home, and it will always smell like an orange covering up a fart. It has no effect on a smelly fart. Especially if that smelly fart came out of Grandma's butt. By the way, it was me. I farted. You're welcome. Get used to it. I'll do it again before you check out.

QUESTION #13: How do I get on the bus? Streetcar? To the mall? Across the street?

ANSWER I GAVE YOU: It's simple. I can give you an area map for the public transit and entrance points for the mall. It's my job to point you in the right direction and explain all there is to see and do in our amazing city.

ANSWER I WANTED TO GIVE YOU: Okay, I understand that public transit in all cities varies and can be very confusing. New Orleans is no different. It's well laid out, and there's an app to help you get from point A to point B. I repeat this answer a million times a day to the point where I want to bang my head on the wall. I'll never be mean about the public transit system. I get confused as hell when I travel. On the other hand, if you don't know how to literally step on a public bus, then we have another problem. Here is your step-by-step guide: wait by the sign, bus stops, doors open, and here is the hard part—you step on. Now here is where it gets really interesting: you pay the bus driver. I know! I just blew your mind. It's the same for the streetcar, except it's on rails. No, there's no middle track. You won't die if you touch the rail. I'm not shitting you. Some people can't even cross the street without directions. You look left, you look right, you put one little foot in front of the other. Please look both ways before you cross the street. The drivers in New Orleans suck serious buttholes. They don't care if you have the right of way. You'll bounce off their car and be nothing but a slick mark on the road. In a battle between man and machine, you will not win. You want to physically go into the mall? You open a glass door and walk through it. Get professional help if these basic tasks cause you anxiety. As the reader, you're probably asking yourself, "Come on, why are you being such an asshole about this?" I mention it because it happens repeatedly. I've had to walk someone across the street and literally open the door to the outlet mall because a guest "couldn't figure it out." No, it wasn't a ninety-five-year-old senile grandma. It was who I thought to be an intelligent mid-thirties woman. Stupidity has no age limit. Shame on me for thinking that it did. The terrified look on her face as I opened the door to the outlet mall only equaled that of someone who was about to walk into a Halloween haunted house. I wanted to scream, "Boo!" but I'm sure she would have crapped her white pants, which she was wearing after Labor Day. Tsk-tsk.

What happened when she wanted to walk in her home? Did she just stand in front of her door and pray hard for it to open on its own? I'd really like to know the answer to both of these questions. I tried really hard not to shake my head at her, but I probably did.

QUESTION #14: Is New Orleans a safe city? Should I stay inside or near the hotel?

ANSWER I GAVE YOU: New Orleans is well policed, and I always feel safe here. With any city, please be cautious of your surroundings. Be observant, walk with a purpose, and stay on the main roads where foot traffic is abundant. I don't suggest walking down a side street, on a dark street, or in an area where you don't feel comfortable. A good rule to remember: the closer you are to the Mississippi River, the safer you'll feel.

ANSWER I WANTED TO GIVE YOU: Did you come here to hide in your hotel room? If you wanted to stay inside all day, then you wasted your trip. New Orleans is a curvy lady. Go explore every inch of her. She does bite, but she loves when you bite back. You'll find something new to discover around every corner. There are hidden courtyards, neighborhood bars, live performances, wine gardens, breweries, and so much more! They're all at your fingertips. Your concierge can help you find your way. Don't be chicken. Get out there and do it all. I hate when people whine about New Orleans being a dangerous city. If you were so scared about coming here for your girls' trip, then maybe you shouldn't have come here. We do not have a zipline over Bourbon Street. We're already a wild-enough city. Yes, it can be dangerous, but so can any city in the world. No, I can't guarantee your safety, and you shouldn't ask me to. What you do while you're away from my desk is your business. I can suggest where to go and where not to go, but it's ultimately your choice. The main thing to remember is not to be a dumbass. If you see a dark spooky street, hear the howl of a banshee, and notice no lights on the street but still see shadows, then don't go down the street. Say no, turn your scared butt around, and run in the other direction. It amazes me how little common sense people have. This is not a B horror movie where the girl runs, trips, breaks her ankle, and then gets gutted by a man in a clown mask. This is New Orleans, and it's hella cool here. If you get lost, ask the first bartender you see. He'll tell you his entire life story, but he'll get you to where you're going. Have fun, and play it safe. Laissez les bons temps rouler!

QUESTION #15: Where is my credit card? My purse? Car keys? Gift bag? My wedding cake? My child? My husband? *(These questions are for the ladies.)*

ANSWER I GAVE YOU: I'm sorry, Rando Guest. The item you're inquiring about has not been turned in to concierge services. If you can provide me with a detailed description of the said item, I'll make sure to give your report to our loss prevention team. They'll take the appropriate action to ensure the item is returned to you, if found. I wish you the best of luck in finding your item.

ANSWER I WANTED TO GIVE YOU: Are you farting kidding me? I'm not the keeper of your lost artifacts. Let's start with the first item on your list. You were foolish enough to leave your credit card lying around in this city? I hope you have your credit card help desk number on speed dial because that plastic bundle of joy has already been maxed out and thrown in the street. In all my years here, I've almost never been asked for an ID to use a credit card. This is a swipe-and-go city. The name on the card can be Susie van Satan, and vendors will sell me anything I want. Someone is enjoying a daiquiri on your dime right now. Why the hell would I have your purse? If you can't keep up with this very important item, then your purse deserves to be stolen. I'm gonna bet a shiny quarter, and let's see if I win. You put your purse on the ground without looping your foot through it, didn't you? Well, guess what? That cute kid who tap-danced in front of you also swiped it. You know that nice lady who tried to sell you a necklace? That was Big-Boobed Bertha, and she just got a purse full of new play toys. Cancel your cards. I hope you have cash in your boob purse for a cab ride home. Silver lining, cabbies will take your cash, no matter how sweaty it is. I have your car keys. Just a second while I concentrate on pushing really, really hard. Please excuse my loud grunts of excruciating pain. Magic. Here they are. Right up my ass! Not them? Wait a minute. That's probably because you gave them to the valet when you were too drunk to remember doing it. Don't drink and drive. It's not cool. Did you hand them to a hard-working young man in a black uniform at the front of the hotel? You're in luck. Did you hand them to anyone else? You're screwed. Good luck getting home. Did you give me a list of wedding guests who should receive your gift bags? You didn't provide one to us? So . . . we're just supposed to know which of the hundreds of wedding guests we have staying here right now to give those to? How cute. I bet you think you're the only blushing bride here, don't you? You expect us to have extrasensory perception? We don't know whom to give your junk drawer gadgets and gizmos to. Your whosits and whatsits are precious, but it doesn't work that way. You give me a list of names, and they get the gift bags. Sounds simple, right? You'd think so. The least you could do is put gift tags on them. You're one of a thousand people having that special wedding moment in New Orleans. Yes, we keep the leftovers, unless you request them back. And yes, I appreciate the cheap mini bottles of champagne. It was nasty, but I drowned it in orange juice. It's your wedding! Spring for the good stuff. Can you tell that brides in general irritate me? Just wait until you read the bridal story in the next chapter. Oh, and that cake thing. That one is totally on you. I don't want anything to do with your frosted pile of red velvet and king cake turd–flavored treat. You think it's the sweetest thing ever, and that's cute. I see dozens of wedding cakes dance through this lobby weekly. I've only been impressed twice. It's not my fault it's lost or looks horrible, so please don't scream at me. Call your baker to find that lost memory, then come to me for an alternate solution. Yes, I know an excellent place for you to buy a cake, and it'll make your mouth water. You lost your kids? How? Tie them to your side. I love children of all ages. I'll do everything I can to find your kid. I'll call the police, run around the lobby, or call out the bloodhounds to find a small child. In today's climate you better have an iron-clasped grip on your small kids. They're precious cargo. I'm not a parent, and the fear of losing my child is why I'm not. This is a city of crowds, and it's very easy to get separated from your loved one. My first question is always, "How old is your child?" and then I quietly go into panic mode. However, when the "child" is old enough to have his or her *own* children, I get annoyed. The kids are twenty-one? They're okay. They're drinking with their friends. They don't want Mom and Dad tagging along. There's this thing called "cool creds," and you're making your kids lose them rapidly. Let them drink and be young. You were that age at one time. Leave them the fart alone. You lost your husband? I'm hiding my smile. This tells me that you lose him often or he runs away from you regularly. I have a bell you can tie on his neck. Will that help? I'm not going to run around the city or even the lobby to look for him, but I'll give you some suggestions. There's a casino down the road. Go look in it. I'm guessing he's dropping a bill and having a blast without you. Earlier in the book, I mentioned a few ladies of the night called sex workers. I'm sorry to say this, but he's lost in their world now. You may also want to haul your caboose to Bourbon Street and peel the shot girls off him. Once they get their claws in him, your kid's college fund will have a zero balance in the morning. While you're at it, check those gay bars. You never know, right? Gay bars are vortexes when you cruise too close. "Straight" men accidentally find themselves pulled into those bars for the drink specials. The "drink specials" are what we'll call it. Yes, I'm internally laughing at you right now. I'm not here to keep track of your husband. I'm not here to locate your plaything or to play with his thing. Is he cute and hung? All bets are off. You think Las Vegas is Sin City? Honey, that desert city has nothing on New Orleans.

QUESTION #16: Did you tell my wife to go shopping? Did you tell my wife to spend money? Did you tell my wife where I was? Did you tell my wife I snuck out? Did you tell my wife I was gambling? Did you tell my wife I was drinking? Did you tell my wife I bought her an expensive present? Did you tell my wife about the expensive restaurant that I booked for us? Did you tell my wife about our special plans? And on, and on, and on . . . *(These questions are for the men.)*

ANSWER I GAVE YOU: I'm sorry, Rando Guest, but I keep all personal information discussed between me and all guests a guarded secret. If you have concerns about your stay, I can have a member of our management team reach out to you soon. I hope you have a wonderful stay.

ANSWER I WANTED TO GIVE YOU: I seriously dislike when people spill the beans about someone else's business or question me about situations. There's a right and a wrong way to work with a concierge. Please trust and believe that we only want the best for you. I'm not a dirty rat. Please don't ask me to be one. I feel that people who intentionally seek to ruin plans should be lined up against a dirty brick wall and biblically stoned with rotten vegetables. Their last dying view of the world should be of you, smiling down at them as you spit in their eye. It has been my experience that concierges are extremely good at keeping secrets. Keeping our mouths shut about everything from a wedding proposal on the rooftop to a simple surprise dinner reservation is our job. If you think we have time to spread gossip about your playtime without the wife, you're sadly mistaken. Unless, of course, it's a real raunchy, chocolate-covered, sex sling, spanking story, and then every concierge in the city is going to hear about it. It's what I call a concierge tabloid moment. Concierges love to share their stories with one another. It's what makes our job fun. We won't use your name, but you'll be famous by the next morning. I purposely grouped all these questions together just for you dudes. Here are your answers. Did I tell your wife where to shop? I probably did, but I honestly don't remember who your wife is. Please don't describe her to me. I've talked to a thousand people today, and everyone starts to blur together. You need to stand out for me to remember you. Just a hint: I remember people by their smiles. The bigger you smile and the nicer you are, the more I like you. The shopping question gets an autopilot answer. There are so many boutiques to buy a unique item in New Orleans that your credit cards will be screaming by the end of your vacation. Was she annoying me? If so, then I admit to sending her as far away from me as possible. I'm not her totally cool new gay best friend, and it's not like she's going to bring me back a cashmere sweater. I don't care where she spends your money. I only care that you support our local economy. You can take home a giant diamond-encrusted crawfish statue with pearls plucked from the depths of the Gulf of Mexico for all I care. Thank you! Did I tell your wife you went out? No. But if you need to sneak out to drink, gamble, or just get away from your wife, then chances are, she shouldn't be your wife. Believe me, I'm there for you, bud. I'd rather help you find a moment of peace than listen to you bitch about how miserable she makes you feel. Men bitch about everything. Society has raised people to believe it's always the woman who complains, and sometimes that's true, but it's men who get real nasty. I don't take sides. I don't care how much either of you drink and how she's always on your nerves. Please go drink alone, gamble, sleep around, or stick your penis in whatever hole you fall into. Have fun with that. Did I spoil the surprise for your wife? That's just mean, and I'd be ashamed to do that to her. The present you bought her, the expensive restaurant, the plans you made, and the thousand other fine details were all me. They were so special that you didn't even bother to arrange for them yourself. I'm offended that you'd second-guess me. You need to have a little faith. You gave me the information, and I did exactly what you couldn't figure out how to do. It's my job, and I love doing it.

Why would I spoil it? However, here's the rub, bro. You said a nice Italian restaurant, and she hates Italian. That's not on me. You should know her better. I bought her flowers, and she's allergic to roses. Don't come to my desk and slam them down, screaming at me. How would I know that? I'm not taking the hit for your lack of knowledge. I'll be nice enough to say how beautiful the flowers are that YOU ordered for her. Does she hate the plans you made? That's funny. I suggested for you to go on a romantic horse-drawn carriage ride, but you wanted to go charter fishing instead. Don't blame me when she complains of bugs and the hot summer heat of New Orleans. Listen, guys, it's simple. Understand this concept. Grow a pair of balls, and just admit to her you messed up. I'm here to help you fix your mistakes. You want an original idea? Do what she wants to do! If that means going to an all-male review, then do it. Let Mega Mike, the ten-inch snake charmer, slap you in the face with his giant manhood. It's not that bad. It may spit on you a little, and that's okay. She'll love you more for the good memories.

QUESTION #17: Damn it. I don't understand where to go! Where do I check in? Why is it such a long walk? Where's the bag man?

ANSWER I GAVE YOU: Good afternoon. You'll find the hotel registration desk directly to the right of concierge services. We do have round-the-clock service for most departments. Do you require assistance with your luggage? It'll be my pleasure to call a bellman to assist you. Have a lovely day, and welcome to New Orleans.

ANSWER I WANTED TO GIVE YOU: You literally walked in and started complaining before looking around. My desk is next to the sign directing guests to the front desk for registration. It's so mind-numbingly clear where the registration desk is located, yet you feel the need to be a puckered asshole before breakfast. I'll answer this one by saying where check-in is not. Check-in is NOT at the bar. In what universe would you walk up to a very busy bartender and expect to get checked into your room? Did the bartender ignore you? Good. Do you blame him? You're in the wrong place. I mean seriously, come on! How moronic do you have to be to think registration is located at the same place we're slinging drinks? The bartender won't give you a room key, clean your room, or spot-lift you in the gym. What he will do is make one hell of a cocktail. Check-in is NOT at the back of the hotel. Why did you roll to the end of a long hallway and take three turns away from the lobby? We don't hide the registration desk in the back of the building next to the public bathrooms. If a hotel offers you a complimentary smell of turds with your registration, walk to another hotel. There are no hidden secrets to finding the desk. Don't make it more difficult than it is. Did you see that huge sign that says, "Bathrooms," with an arrow pointing in that direction? It truly means that you're heading toward the bathrooms and not a secret VIP area, unless you're into water sports. Check-in is NOT at concierge services. Yes, there is a huge sign here, too, that says, "Concierge Services," and this may surprise you, but it's exactly that. True, there are concierge services desks where the concierge prefers to register a VIP guest. Are you a VIP? No. Keep walking, rando. Did you listen to the living, breathing person at the front door who greeted you? He was the guy you ignored and walked by with your nose in the air. You acted too good to say hello, and now you're lost. One rule to staying in any hotel: Say hello to everyone who says hello to you. Don't be that asshole. Congratulations! You arrived at your magic registration desk destination. What's the problem now? You're complaining about the ten-foot walk or the fact that you carried your luggage all the way to this remote registration desk? Calm down, drama queen. You're acting like you traveled across a bloody battleground, fighting vicious demons. I was standing right here. Your car is literally far enough away that I could spit on it. I should spit on it. The valet can't drive into our lobby. It's as close as it physically can be without running over Grandma. I also heard the bellman ask whether you needed assistance with your luggage, and you declined it. Don't come back to the concierge services desk and lie that he didn't offer his service. We have cameras everywhere for your security, and we see all. Big Brother is watching you. True, there are shit valets and bellmen at every hotel who will never speak to you. We can see them, too. They won't be employed here for much longer if they don't help make your stay incredible. However, I'm guessing you declined because you didn't want to tip him a dollar for each bag. Don't be cheap. You don't know where to go after checking in? That's because you didn't listen to the front desk agent explain the property. You were too busy rudely texting or talking on your phone to pay attention. They told you the hours of the restaurant, where the gym was, and how to use your keys. I'll laugh when you step on the elevator and can't figure out how to operate it. It's not broken; you're just too lazy to read the big sign that says, "Insert Card Here." You don't want me to step into the elevator and show you. Why? I'll crop-dust every inch of that space before I step out, and you deserve it. You're welcome. I told you I'd fart again. Here's my suggestion to every guest, and it works amazingly well every time. Look up from your phone and pay attention. There are signs everywhere, and there are tons of smiling people waiting to help you. All you need to do is smile and say hello.

QUESTION #18: Where's the bathroom?

ANSWER I GAVE YOU: Good afternoon. The bathrooms are located down the hallway past the restaurant. You'll make two turns, and they'll be on the right. Make it a great day!

ANSWER I WANTED TO GIVE YOU: Hello, Polly Poopy Pants. Look around and read the damn signs. I know that I glazed over this in question #17, but I feel the need to expand on this question. When I say, "Make it a great day!" what I meant to say was "Enjoy your time dropping that turd baby off at the pool!" It's the only question that genuinely irritates me so much that I feel the need to walk outside and scream. My personal hell when I die will be sitting at a concierge desk answering this question every day all day. I answer it so often that I've started to change my accent just for the hell of it. I've said it with a British, Scottish, Australian, German, Asian, Hispanic, and every other accent you can think of. Yes, I was bad at it. My favorite accent is a super-slow gay Southern accent. That one always gets a laugh. I've changed what I say and how I say this answer a million times. Yet I still have not found the perfect way to say it without grinding my teeth. Where's the bathroom? Excuse me, the bathroom? You got a bathroom somewhere? Where's the shitter? Ugh! Again, there is a giant farting sign right in front of your vapid, constipated face. I hate this question, but everyone takes a dump. When you gotta go, you gotta go. I get it. I have baby wipes for accidents. Wipe front to back. Wash your hands. Don't shake mine afterward. Can you do me a big favor and please pass this information along to people who don't read this book? Throw your paper towels in the wastebasket and not next to it. If you miss the trash can at home, do you leave your trash on the floor? I doubt it. This is your home for the next few days, so treat it that way. The housekeeping staff will appreciate it.

QUESTION #19: Where's a good place to eat?

ANSWER I GAVE YOU: This is a foodie city. We have something for everyone. There are nearly 150 restaurants in the downtown area, with 900+ restaurants in the New Orleans metro area. You can spend a lifetime here and never eat at half of our amazing, award-winning restaurants. Let's narrow the choices down for you with a few questions. I want to suggest the best place for you to eat.

ANSWER I WANTED TO GIVE YOU: This is the number-one asked question about the city besides restroom location. Every restaurant is unique with its own flavor and delicious flair. This city is food porn for foodies. You can die from overeating here. We're a walking, talking, eating, "sweat it out and do it all over again" type of a city. I love it. Don't ask me where's a good place to eat because they're all great, lip-smacking, belly-slapping places to eat. Your head will spin by all the options I can give you. Do your concierge and yourself a favor: carefully look at a list of restaurants in New Orleans before you get here. Decide on your top five, and call us in advance. We'll do our best to make it happen. I'm not being overly dramatic. Seriously, call us a week or two in advance. I feel bad when a guest wants to eat at a special restaurant and there's no table available. The restaurant is fully committed, which means you ain't getting in unless there's a cancellation, and that's rare. Granted, I'm damn good at miracles, but I'm not clairvoyant. You're not impressing anyone by being lazy and trying to make a dinner reservation at the last minute.

The family-owned restaurants have been here for a hundred-plus years. Don't ask me if you should eat there because I'll say yes, every time. Go eat there! The restaurant scene in New Orleans is not only delicious but competitive. Each restaurant strives to be the best. They have signature dishes that are not-to-miss staples on their menu. Try them all. My tip to you would be to go, sit at the bar, and eat that signature dish. You'll not be disappointed. Not having a table is not the end of the world. You're here for the experience, not the table. If you really want to do your tummy right, then hop around eating appetizers at every place you want to go. You can make it a Sunday Funday of food porn heaven. The other tip is to eat at a real soul food kitchen. You need to get out of the French Quarter and take a cab to that dirty diner that serves all its meals in a white Styrofoam container. Those cheap white containers are overflowing with sweet, sweet deliciousness. If you barely tip them to the side, you're getting a lap full of stewed cabbage sauce. I'll lick it off your lap. I dare you to walk by my desk. You've been warned, my little cabbage-dipped morsel. New Orleans restaurants are so good, you'll want to slap your momma, your neighbor's momma, and your neighbor's momma's momma. If you come back here without crawfish cornbread for me, I'll kick you in the nuts or cooch or whatever you have dangling down there. Don't do it.

QUESTION #20: Is there a bartender working?

ANSWER I GAVE YOU: Yes. There's a bartender on duty. He may have stepped in the back to retrieve a food order for a guest or a stock item for the bar. Please give me a moment to let him know you're here. Thank you for your patience, and I'll be right back.

ANSWER I WANTED TO GIVE YOU: No. The entire bar is set up for service with no bartender on duty. The guests sitting there with drinks in hand must have served themselves. It's a free-for-all bar! Didn't you know that every hotel in New Orleans has fully stocked bars set up for you to serve yourself? You're a dumbass. Yes, there's a bartender. Sit down, and wait for him to come back. Guests are so impatient when it comes to their alcohol. I understand. You walked up to the bar, you saw no one standing there, and you had an emotional breakdown. It's a traumatic experience for you, but calm the fart down. Please use a nugget of common sense before you ask this question. A better way to say this is "I'd like to order a drink. Can you tell the bartender I'm waiting to order?" Yes, I absolutely can. All bartenders in New Orleans stay busy and rarely get the chance to breathe. They're not only running food orders for the ten other people at the bar, but they're stocking, getting ice, retrieving glassware and snacks, turning the TV channel, answering the phone, replacing the beer tap, and doing a hundred other things. I know you only see a snapshot, but excuse the bartenders if they're not behind the bar at the very moment you step up. Try this revolutionary idea out. Strike up a conversation with someone at the bar. It's a great way to make a new friend. If the bartender isn't back in five minutes, then please come talk to me. Don't scream profanities at me or expect me to mix a drink for you. It's not my job. It will be my pleasure to find the bartender, but when you assume that there's just no one working, I get irritated. You know what they say: assumption makes an ass out of you. Your being an asshole will not make me find the bartender faster. It will only help me decide on how much longer to make you wait.

QUESTION #21: Why can't you fix the water outage or stop the boil water advisory?

ANSWER I GAVE YOU: I'm sorry for the inconvenience. This is a city-wide problem that our local government is working to correct. The Sewage and Water Board of New Orleans does give us frequent updates, and we'll inform you of news as it's released. We can provide you with bottled water for basic needs until the water outage is corrected or the boil water advisory has been lifted.

ANSWER I WANTED TO GIVE YOU: There is a special corner of hell reserved just for you. You're the only person in the city whom this is affecting. The mayor is personally turning the wrench. Guess what? We're all in the same situation. I'm not Jesus, and I can't create clean drinking water out of wine. Your New Orleans baptism can wait. This is an issue that happens now and then, and all you can do is suffer with us. Would you rather drink tainted water and get a brain-eating bacteria? Do you think I'm making that shit up to shut you down? I'm not. Look it up; it's a thing. The water is shut off, and the advisory is in place for your protection. No, I will not give you a free room, a discount on your rate, or a free foot rub. It's not our fault, and we're just as pissed about it as you are. Stop being an annoying crybaby. The hotel has it worse. We must listen to you whine because you can't brush your teeth or have a sip of water before bed. We can't drink the water either. Your brilliant ass crapped in a toilet that can't be flushed. We get it, but don't crap and then blame us because the smell is bad enough to peel the paint off the bathroom wall. Here's a chance for you to practice your patience or, better yet, go get a cold beer from that bartender you can't seem to find. Enjoy the brew.

That's it, folks! Those are my all-time top twenty-one favorites. There's never a shortage of dumb questions, and I never have a shortage of dumb answers. Yes. I have dumb answers. I'm not Einstein. If it made this list, it wasn't a smart one. I could've written an entire book just on the questions. Do you see me ferociously typing at my desk? I'm typing the best dumb questions into my notes section while we're talking. Keep them coming because I need the material. My last and final suggestion is to stop and think before you speak. This is something that parents have been saying to their numbskull kids since the dawn of time, but it's the truth. My dad would hit me on the back of the head when I asked a dumb question. I won't hit you, but the thought did cross my mind. I hope this section helps you during your vacation. If any of these apply to you, then may God have mercy on your soul. Are you ready for the real juice of this book? The crazy, funny, fantastic conversations are next! This is going to be fun. Did you hear me squeal a little? I totally did.

DoodleMaBob by Joshua Carpenter, *Art Says What?*

CHAPTER THREE

CONVERSATIONS WITH YOUR CONCIERGE

E very concierge's life is full of interesting conversations with guests. Some build a sense of relationship, friendship, and endless laughter. These are the conversations I love the best. Then there are times when the conversation is so derailed by a guest's stupidity that it's hard for me to keep an emotionless facial expression. Some guests are 100 percent hopeless, no matter how you spin it. The lines between good and bad can often become blurred. I'm guilty of assuming the worst but hoping for the best. I try very hard to treat everyone the same, but it's not always easy. I've caught myself reaching for the good ones, who are increasingly rare, and running from the bad ones, who overwhelming predominate. Hope is escaping. I'm holding tight to the last thread.

I have had some of the most intellectual and motivating conversations with people from all over the world. I once spoke with a lady who helped lead a women's movement for equality in New York City, a lady who started a giant cookie company with a nickel and a dream, and a man who wrote inspirational children's stories for low-income families. Every day I'm lucky enough to talk to people way more educated than I am and learn from their experiences.

A good conversation is easy to have if you're open to having one. Everyone loves to connect and talk about his or her life. Everybody's viewpoint on life is different, but in one way or another they're relatable to your own. I remember talking to a couple from Canada who were so fascinating that I felt sad after they left my desk. I could have talked to them for days. They gifted me with a birdcage, which still hangs in my kitchen window today, but, more important, they gifted me with friendship. Shout-out to you, Don and Narjes. I can't wait to visit Calgary.

I collected the following conversations from some of these amazing and not-so-amazing people. They've changed my life for the better. They've also taught me how not to be a total asshole to the human race. I love most people but not all. My most difficult challenge is how to stop myself from bursting out in laughter in front of them. I'll have one great educational conversation, and then five ridiculous ones rear their ugly heads. These are the ones that I couldn't forget even if I tried. They're burned into my memory. They have either scarred my damned soul or filled my heart with love. They roll around in my noggin, morphing into something fun and new every time I relive them. The stories slowly change over time, like a bad gossip chain. They take on a life of their own. I try to write them down as soon as they happen, but sometimes I'm just too damn busy. I want them to remain rooted in the core of what they are before I forget what they were.

There are many things I could gripe about, but the top of the list is when guests have no respect, possess no decency toward other people, or don't listen to the advice of someone who is only trying to help. I have a great capacity for driving a conversation forward, leading it to where it needs to go, and ending every conversation with a smile. However, I'm the proverbial "You can lead a horse to water, but you can't make him drink it" concierge. The horse being the stubborn guests. No matter how hard I try, those damn horses won't drink the juice

These stories are about a wide range of different people from different places living very different realities and running a very different race than the rest of us. You'll find in my stories that offending people and loving people are spread out on a case-by-case basis. Some of the people have no common sense or way too much for their own good. Some people have no decency, and others make me look like a huge asshole. I enjoy looking at life as if it's a big bag of assorted donuts. Keep taking small bites of life experiences, and you'll eventually get the flavor you want. Enjoy!

BARISTA I AM NOT

I work very close to our hotel's coffee stand. The stand is an obvious place for a coffee location and is centrally located where even a brain-dead goblin can find it. Behind it stands a very happy barista ready to take your every order. It's her job to make sure you get the best cup of New Orleans coffee that the city has to offer. We're famous for our chicory coffee, and we like to show it off. The pastries might not be so fresh, but the coffee rocks. It's New Orleans cocaine, and you always come back for more.

I'm not a barista. I don't want to be one. You don't want me to make you a fancy cup of joe. However, I get asked for one about five times a year. There's always a snarky jackhole who thinks I can magically poop out a cup of coffee. Trust me on this fact, I can't. Do you see the line of guests at the coffee counter? You need to wait to get that delicious cup of New Orleans cocaine, just like everyone else. Lick this flavor up, and enjoy every drop.

Terrible Texting Tiffany was my first experience with this phenomenon. I just don't get it. Like, totally to the max. Look around, Tiff . . . God! Tiff, for short, walks up to me holding her phone for dear life. She's two-thumb typing furiously away like she's single-handedly warning the world that the end is near. She never looks up at me. Tiff is one blonde dye job away from being bald. She has fake pointed tits that are pulled so far up, they're almost touching her chin. Her face is pulled back so tight that sight must be a challenge. To top it off, she's wearing white thigh-high boots with pink laces. I look her up and down and wonder what in crazy hell is about to fall out of her collagen-filled lips. What she says makes me laugh out loud. Tiff doesn't look up from her phone. I doubt she can hear me giggle since her ears are tucked behind her head.

Tiffany: My name is Tiff. Charge it to my room. I want a tall vanilla peppermint-flavored Guatemalan hand-squeezed bean, half a double-shot espresso French drip, triple-dipped chocolate-covered mint wafer, screw me hard up the tight privileged ass while donkey punching my sister in a cardboard refrigerator box . . . and I need it RIGHT NOW!

I have no clue what she asked for. It sounded like a code during wartime, where coffee was the soldier and she was the five-star general. This gave me a better appreciation for baristas, and I never ordered another difficult drink from a barista again. Please give me drip coffee, hold the spit, and I'll walk away. As I wait for her to realize where she is, I am having several violent thoughts. I'll bet I could punch her in the crotch, and she'd never figure out that it was me. It would be a drive-by crotch punching, while I screamed, "He ran that way, Tiff!" There's a long pause, followed by a sigh. I say nothing.

Tiffany: Did you hear me? I want a blah blah blah blah, flying almond cheese croissant, type, type, huff, grunt, fart, spewing irrelevant information at me, blah, blah blah. Foot tap, foot tap, tap, tap, tap again.

Don't stomp your tiny fake footwear at me! I wait, not saying a word. I don't expect much from people. I'm an easy guy. I do expect Tiff to look up at me. Please make eye contact with the person you assume is serving you coffee. I'll spit on everything you own if you don't. Please. Give me that small ounce of respect. I also enjoy peeing on stuff. Don't think I won't hike my leg up on you. There isn't anything I can say to her that won't sound dickish.

I patiently wait until some miracle voice in her too-tight stretched face tells her to pay attention to me. Hey there, lady, are you done saving the world? Tiff finally looks up with an irritated, shocked expression on her face. I have an equally annoyed look on my face. Has she just been teleported to some distant land of Conciergia or finally realized that reality has caught up with her? I see a real-life boy when I look in the mirror. The only thing Tiff sees is a green-skinned alien with no coffee for her.

Me: Good morning, ma'am.

I stress the old **ma'am** word in a thick country accent because she obviously has an aversion to aging. I don't like Tiff. She's annoying. I want to hold a flame up to her face and watch the plastic melt like a crayon. On second thought, Tiff will probably explode in a screaming ball of fire. I don't want Tiff taking me to hell with her. I'm going out on a limb to guess that her version of hell will be standing in a long line for coffee and never reaching the barista to order. Maybe an open flame around here is not a very good idea.

Tiffany: Where's my coffee? Hello!

WTF? Bitch, do you see a coffee stand around me? This is a desk with two chairs and a phone. Where do you think I'm hiding the coffee? I look around to compose myself. I want to make sure I'm not getting punked or secret-shopped. Tiff is not in on the joke. I look back at her with a very big smile on my face. She looks at me like I have just taken a shit on her long-haired cat.

Me: The barista who is standing directly behind you, across from this desk, at the coffee stand, can help you with that order. This is Concierge Services, and sadly we don't serve coffee here, but I sure would love a cup.

Giggle, giggle. I don't get a giggle back from Terrible Texting Tiffany. I have never wanted to punch someone in the face so bad. The sneer emanating from her wide face is deadly. She doesn't speak, only raises her eyebrow. Her ability to raise an eyebrow shocks me. With that much Botox in her face, I doubt she can express any emotion. There is an awkward, uncomfortable silence where I can see her gears moving. She is plotting my demise.

Me: I'll be happy to direct you to a local coffee shop if the one directly behind you, across from this desk, at the coffee stand, does not have the coffee you wish.

I fracture the black heart that Tiff has in her cold, beating, fake boobs. I push a knife through her chest by not having coffee at my desk. I enjoy it. Tiff is trying to save the world, one text at a time! How dare I not have a full coffee bar at my fingertips? I just made her realize that civilization is not ending. There is someone other than her standing on this Earth.

I'll do everything I can to build your memory of New Orleans, but I'm not willing to satisfy your every coffee fantasy.

Tiffany: Ugh! If I must order from there, I will.

Me: Have a nice day, and enjoy our lovely city.

I know what you're all thinking. Did Terrible Texting Tiffany make it across the lobby to the coffee stand? Yes, Tiff waited all of thirty seconds and then walked away. She huffed and puffed without blowing out a cheekbone and walked that marathon of fifty feet. I saw her nearly run into a small child because her nose was planted firmly in her phone. She was really fingering the hell out of that thing. The least she could have done was buy it dinner and offer it a cigarette. I guess waiting to be helped or being a decent human being to others was not her way of saving the day. She power-lifted her fun bags, adjusted her horns, swung her demon tail over one arm, and then rode her broom out of the lobby.

Tiffany: I hate this city!

I had narrowly escaped being a barista for the first time in my concierge career. I thought this was going to be a once-in-a-lifetime occurrence, but it turned out to be a situation I would deal with often. I became a professional at spotting the coffee monsters looking for our famous New Orleans cocaine. I even made a list of local coffee shops with beignets. The guests would now have everything they needed. It didn't work. I never got another lady quite like Tiff, but I did get others. It became so common that one story wasn't enough. Bless it.

CONFUSED CARL AND THE COFFEE CONUNDRUM

Poor Carl. He was a portly, slow little fella as round as Santa and as bald as a bowling ball. I guessed his age to be around mid-fifties, and he was always smiling. I enjoyed our conversations and look back on them fondly. Carl was smart but couldn't find his way out of a wet paper bag, even with a tour guide holding his hand. The brilliant thing about Carl was that he could laugh at himself. He was a nervous laugher, which made him laugh even more. It's okay, Carl, I'm a nervous laugher, too.

I remember that I was in an exceptionally great mood that morning. It's not true for every morning, but I have my moments. I look up and see this man slowly and very carefully moving into my territory. Carl has a sideway smile and is creeping up on me as if I'm something dangerous to get near. I don't bite. Carl starts with a stutter, and I immediately smile and widen my eyes. This will be another good coffee conversation, or is Carl going to throw me a curveball? Bring it on, Carl.

Carl: Ummm, excuse . . . uh . . . excuse me?

Me: How may I help you today, sir?

Carl: I'm not sure . . . uh . . . sure how to ask this . . . uh . . . this question?

I lean in, smirk nicely, and motion to my chair for him to have a seat. Yes, there are several ways of smirking without being an asshole about it. There is a pattern to the way each person speaks, and if you're really paying attention, you can spot the pattern. If a guest is stammering his words within the first sentence, then that guest will be standing there for at least the next ten minutes to get his point across to me. I'm prepared for a long talk with Carl.

Me: I assure you, sir, that I've been asked just about everything under the sun. What's your question? I'll have an answer to throw back at you. If I can't answer it, I know a lot of other concierges I can reach out to.

Carl takes a seat and looks a little less nervous. He puts his hands in his lap and grips his pants tightly. Sweat begins to bead on his brow. I am 99 percent sure he is going to ask for an adult diaper or something that's so embarrassing that he doesn't want to ask me, but he really needs to ask me. You laugh? I've had a guest ask for an adult diaper and be upset I didn't have one in my magic drawer of tricks. Carl takes a deep breath and then bombards me with coffee-related questions. I feel the force hit me like a hurricane. Slow down, Carl.

Carl: I have never . . . uh . . . never stayed at a place this fancy. I . . . I don't understand. Ummm . . . I mean . . . I just don't get it. Why is there a coffee machine in my room, but it's not plugged in? Is . . . uh . . . is it broke? How does it work? Do I have to pay . . . pay for it? If so, how much is each bag? What is the difference between ordering coffee in the restaurant and . . . uh . . . ordering it at the coffee stand? Do I have to sit . . . sit down and eat, or can I just get coffee? Can I get it to go . . . go . . . go from the restaurant or just the coffee stand? Do I have to order off the menu, or can I just get . . . get a regular cup of coffee? I . . . I am just so confused. I . . . I am not used to this. What do I do?

Ding. Ding. Ding. Carl is an extremely obsessive-compulsive man, and so am I. Carl is also a man who overanalyzes everything, and so am I. Carl is a man who likes to know all the answers and options before deciding, and so am I. To say the least, I get where Carl is coming from. Breathe. It's a learned trait for some people, and it's not easy when you're in a new environment. There are times when even the simplest task seems like you're scaling a mountain with a thin rope that's on the verge of snapping.

Me: You sound just like me. Let's tackle these questions one at a time in a very quick Cliff Notes version. I'm easily confused, and the last thing I want to do is confuse you more. You ready?

Carl takes another deep breath and grips the arms on the chair tightly. I straighten my bow tie. I'm ready to do this. It's that feeling you get when you're playing a video game and you're stuck at one difficult point. You've tried repeatedly but just can't get past that point in the game. You've cursed, kicked your dog, and sworn that if you don't get past it this time, then you're done with this farting game forever. You can do it! You just need to barrel through headfirst and have faith. That's just what I do. Don't kick your dog. It's not cool. Your dog will hate you.

Me: You'll need to plug in the coffee machine and follow the directions. The coffee is free, and it's delicious. I can help you figure it out, if you want. I don't mind stretching my legs to assist you. The only difference between the restaurant and the coffee stand is simple. In the restaurant, you can sit down to enjoy a delicious cup of New Orleans joe in a ceramic mug. You don't have to order anything else, and I enjoy the people watching. I'll tell the server the first cup is on me. If you overhear anything interesting, come back and report all the good details. I love a good story. At the coffee stand you can order and go. Grab a hot cup, and hit the streets to start sight-seeing. I can also take care of that for you. I don't leave this desk often, but I don't mind going for a walk with a friend. I take care of my friends.

Carl: Wow! You're really good at your job!

I notice that he didn't stutter. Am I good at my job? The only thing I did was answer a few simple questions for poor Carl. They were not the most professional answers, but they were the answers he needed to hear. The key? I made him feel comfortable about asking something that other people may have thought was asinine. Carl is not a stupid person. He's someone whose mind works a little differently than others'. Someone a lot like me. It would have been too easy to make fun of confused Carl. The man just needed that little bit of kindness.

Me: You're welcome, sir. I'm here to assist with all your needs. Please feel free to come talk to me anytime you want.

Carl: Thank you. I'll be back later today.

Me: Have a nice day, and enjoy our lovely city.

Confused Carl came back to report every single detail while on vacation. I was so proud of him. He got lost in the city several times, called me for directions, and had an amazing trip. He was staying with us for three days, and we must have talked for hours while he was here. He came back the following year and the year after and the year after that. He checked off everything on his New Orleans wish list. His past visit was his last visit. I'll miss you, Confused Carl. I've never answered so many questions so quickly with such vigor as I did with poor Confused Carl. He's one of a kind. Why can't every guest be a Confused Carl?

SNOTTY McSNOTTERSON LEARNS TO FLY

You're not a magical, mythical flying unicorn. Trust me on this. I like to explain directions with a map and a highlighter in hand. I always give a detailed way to a location with street signs, mileage, landmarks, and more. The guest will still fight me tooth and nail on the information. Today's society relies so much on smart phone map technology that most people have lost touch with the fact that a direct line is not always the best route.

There was a time in our history when paper maps were all the rave. I don't know why people look at them now like they're relics of a forgotten, long-lost civilization. Maps are amazing at helping you find your way around a city you've never been to before. New Orleans is a city with a river running through the middle of it; you may need a paper map. Use it. These fantastical things called rivers have these fancy man-made things called bridges or ferries that you must use to get to the other side of the river. Unless you're a magical, mythical flying unicorn, then you need to cross the river via a bridge or a ferry.

This one lady named Snotty fought me on how to get to where she was going. I wasted ten minutes of my precious time explaining directions to her, and all I got was a dumb blank stare back. I finally agreed with her and gave up the fight. With a wave of my hand and a shit-eating grin, I said, "Have a nice bike ride." I did make a friend from this conversation, and that's the best reward at the end of any difficult conversation.

Snotty walks up with a better-than-thou attitude right out of the dirty gate. She's with a group of friends who look like rejects from a failed sorority comedy sitcom. I'm guessing she's trying to impress them with her all-knowing personality. I can tell she's going to talk to me like I'm beneath her, but I always give a person the benefit of the doubt. It's my job to help the guests, even if I think they'll turn out to be a super-snotty, dripping little twat of distaste and ill repute.

Snotty: We're going on a bike ride, and we need to get to this location on my phone. It says that it's only half a mile away. What is the best way to get there?

If you're waving your phone around and demanding to know how to get somewhere, then you already know how to get there. Snotty is making sweet, sweet love to her phone. No one will ever give her an answer that's better than her hand-held, battery-operated boyfriend. Snotty is testing me and being a total mean girl about it. She wants me to screw up, and she'll point it out when I do. Don't go out of your way to make me look inferior to you. That's rude. Snotty can take her outdated eighties-fashion mean girl posse and leave. I know her game and that shit don't fly with me.

Me: That location is half a mile away as the crow flies, but, unfortunately, you'll need to cross the river to get there. The main bridge is for motor vehicles only. Please take this city map with you. It'll help you along your journey. Follow Canal Street to the Canal Street Ferry, where you will cross the river to Algiers Point. The ferry is a lovely ride across the Mississippi River, then it's a nice bike ride to your final destination—just over a mile from the ferry landing.

Of course, I say this with my nicest professional voice. The whole time I'm giving her directions, she's rolling her eyes and looking at her phone. I honestly can give two shits about what I'm saying to Snotty. If her eyes roll back any farther in her skull, they'll roll out of her ass. I'm careful that everything I say is perfect. I can immediately feel her compulsion to act better than everyone around her. She's the type of guest who will complain even if you're right because she's not. I make her look stupid with the correct answer. I do this in front of her friends, and she's not going to have that. I'm smiling big to her friends, and I may even wink a little. They know she's being an ignorant bloody twit. There's more to the story here.

Snotty: That just doesn't make any sense. It shows right here that it's half a mile away. We want to go on a good bike ride, and this looks like the best path to take.

I can hear the know-it-all condemnation building in Snotty's voice. Her nostrils are flaring like a charging bull with a summer cold. I'm right, and Snotty is not.

Me: Yes, ma'am, I agree with you. That's the direct line. However, that doesn't change the fact that there is a river between us and that destination. The best way to get to that location is by ferry. The path I've mapped out for you is excellent. The bike trail along the levee is lovely, and I highly suggest it. I can also point out a few great stopping points along your journey. I suggest stopping at this store and this store, this bar for a drink, this restaurant for yummies. Don't miss the historic courthouse, and sit on the waterfront when you're ready to rest. Would you and your friends enjoy that?

Snotty looks like she's about to internally combust. I love to add a little sass when it's a group of girlfriends. I like to use the eyebrow raise, pursed lips, and a gay lisp trick. She gives me a blank look like I am attempting to explain the mysteries of the universe. I know this city better than the back of my hand. Her friends start laughing behind her back. Girl, you're not going to impress anyone with your crappy attitude. Snotty is too old for this shit. She needs to stop trying to relive her long forgotten, snotty, wannabe-popular high school days when she dreamed of a stinky pinky from the star quarterback and only got the fat thumb from the head band geek.

Snotty: You're no help. We'll find it on our own. I have a phone that's more willing to show us the correct route than you are!

Me: Have a nice bike ride.

Snotty stomps away, pissed off. Her friend proudly strides up to me. She has a gorgeous face, framed with flowing red hair and curves that could kill. Her smile can snuff out the dark and light up the world. She has an old Hollywood bombshell look and a very intoxicating essence. She leans in with her whole body to talk. She has a deep sultry voice that you instantly fall in love with. There's always one friend who's down to earth and super cool in any group. She was listening to what I tried to explain to Snotty. More important, she comprehends the fact that there is a freaking river between us and the destination. This is the lady you want to be best friends with. She's the leader of the pack, and she'll devour you.

Bombshell: Please excuse her, she's not that bright. Can you please give me that city map you were showing her? I'll make sure we use the ferry to get there.

Shade. This girl just threw shade all up in Snotty's face. I love it. I love when a guest gives me that little wink and a big smile back. She knows I've been sitting here for ten hours. I've dealt with people like Snotty all day but can't say anything more than a cleverly worded comment. Girl, you must have been a concierge in another life. Can you be my best friend? You can come sit next to me any day. I was hoping she would slam Snotty again because it made me giggle. It's nice when someone else says what you want to say, but you can't. Damn cat gets my tongue all the damn time. I love when people defend hospitality workers from rude people. It's the right and decent thing to do. Check that bitch's attitude at the door for me.

Me: Of course, I have a thousand maps. I'll highlight the route. I wish every guest was as nice as you.

I throw a sideways stank eye at Snotty McSnotterson, hiss, and spit venom in her general direction. Bombshell then whispers to me, and I whisper back.

Bombshell: Thank you, and I'm sorry for her. She's not really with us, honey.

Me: It's okay. I talk to a guest like her every day.

Bombshell: We may leave her on the other side of the river if she keeps this up. I don't approve of her attitude. I'm sure the other ladies don't either. You don't worry about it, sweetie. We got you covered.

Me: Do you need floaties or a life vest? I can also find rope.

We both chuckle, and little tears of laughter form in her green-colored eyes. She cuts her gaze over to the little group of mean girls and winks. I don't think these mean girls are so mean now. They're guilty by association. I admit I was wrong for judging them when they didn't deserve it. I wonder if that little wink was a hidden cue to the other girls that she got the real scoop. Are they plotting to throw Snotty overboard, bike and all? Was the suggestion of rope a precognitive ability I'm just now discovering? What if that comes true? I didn't commit the crime, and I'm not doing the time. However, I'd totally have a glass of prison wine and talk shit about Snotty. It's what I do best.

Bombshell: I like you. Have a good day, and thank you.

Me: It was my pleasure. I'm here all day to assist. Come back and see me again.

Bombshell: Have a great day, sugar!

Me: Have a nice day, and enjoy our lovely city.

The red bombshell walked away to the sound of ragtime music playing in my head, and every sexy step she took was profound and beautiful. I made a friend for that one moment in time, and I'm a better person for it. Over the next couple of days, the number of ladies hanging out with Snotty dropped to zero. Snotty was sitting in the lobby one morning drinking coffee with a mean-looking snarl on her face. One of the ladies saw her, turned around, and walked the other way. Another of the ladies ducked behind a potted palm tree. She played hide-and-seek until Snotty was looking the other way, then she made a mad dash for the exit. It made me laugh. The level of disgust that Snotty evoked was epic. Did she realize that her "friends" were avoiding her? Why didn't she change her nasty attitude? It was obvious to everyone. You can't change a zebra's stripes, and she was the zebra. I cornered one of the other ladies the next day. My curiosity was piqued, and I had to get all the details on this girls' trip. The mean girl group was here on a work trip. They were tolerating her to be professional. When the work function was over, all bets were off. They didn't need to be nice or even socialize with Snotty anymore. She was on her own.

I said good morning professionally every time Snotty walked near my desk. She would stomp by like a scolded child, and my greetings were always met with silent side glare. Bombshell must have said something to Snotty because she didn't treat me badly again for the rest of her stay. She didn't acknowledge my existence either. I'll take that as a win. I'd rather be ignored than talked down to any day. I don't have a cold, unfeeling heart. I did slightly feel bad for her, but, like gas, it passed very quickly. Goodbye, Snotty McSnotterson. I hope you learned how to fly. I'm a magical, mythical flying unicorn, and my wings are glorious.

THE KARMA OF
MR. MIAMI DOUCHEBAG

I understand that humanity is a mixed bag of assholes. There's an asshole out there for every occasion. They come in all shapes, colors, and sizes. They're messy and dirty, while a few are surprisingly clean but assholes all the same. This is a fact of life. You'll experience an asshole at any job, but hotel assholes are a special lot.

I was lucky enough to experience the blinding stench of an exceptionally rare asshole. He was that one asshole whom everyone immediately hates just for opening his pungent, foul-smelling hole. If there were an asshole contest, he would win the gold medal every time. He was that one asshole who licks his own ass because he thinks it tastes like spiced rum sauce poured over bananas. Mr. Miami Douchebag was that asshole for me. He stands out from all the other assholes I've had the pleasure of sniffing. Don't sniff assholes; it's stinky.

Mr. Miami Douchebag was a rich, entitled Latino prick. Yes, I'm going to talk shit about this *horchata*-flavored pile of poop. My mother is Latino, and I've always felt that I can talk about my own people and still despise everyone else equally. Mr. Douchebag was in town because of a hurricane barreling toward Florida. He was a tall, leather-tanned piece of dried-up beef jerky. He thought because he drove a BMW and wore a cheap Rolex on his barbarian wrist that I would be impressed. I was not. Mr. Miami Douchebag thought he could come into my hotel and throw poo on me. You may look like a gorilla, but don't act like one. He pissed me off so bad that I went for a walk around the building to smoke a cigarette. I'm not a smoker. Mr. Miami Douchebag can travel the express train to Hades holding his tiny banana, and I couldn't care less. Foreshadowing, karma is a mean bitch.

Mr. Douchebag storms in and slams his hand down on my desk. He points out the door and screams at me in this Miami Latino dialect that only a puckered asshole could have. He then spits poo from his dirty lips to the edge of my seat. I gracefully dodge it with the flair of a mixed martial artist. He would be attractive, if he didn't work out to the point of bursting open. I can't help but stare at the roadmap of veins that travels down his neck and arms. Mr. Douchebag has rock-hard man boobs bigger than Big-Boobed Bertha, and his legs look like two twigs tied to a bowling pin. It's called leg day. Look into it. He doesn't intimidate me. I've been yelled at before, and I know when it's about to happen. I'm ready for whatever bullshit he's about to throw at me.

Mr. Douchebag: I'm a guest here. I just got a ticket outside on the street, and I'm not paying it. What are you going to do? I can't believe this! I'm so mad right now!

No shit? Your gorilla-size ass parked illegally on the street in a space clearly marked by a meter. You expect me to fix your ticket just because you're a guest here? I'm internally laughing at you right now. Did I park your car there? Why would you assume you could park there and not pay? Did you think the New Orleans police force wouldn't ticket you because you have a Florida license plate? That's reason to ticket you more! We're about as famous for our parking tickets as we are for Mardi Gras. The meter maids are vicious. They'll tear you apart, one ticket at a time. They don't give a shit who you are. You're driving a BMW. Cha ching! Money in the city bank. They're like hungry vultures, waiting at the meter for it to expire, and then they ticket your vehicle the second it does, laughing the whole time. Don't argue with a meter maid. You will not win. The only thing they're required to say is, "I alrets printed yo ticket! You too late, boo boo. Call da office!" Kiki could care less about your ticket. You're illegally parked. Kiki has a quota to hit. You're just one more ticket toward that quota.

Me: I'm sorry you received a ticket, sir. The parking meters are clearly marked, and tickets can cost up to $75 per violation, depending on where you parked. Would you like the number to the City of New Orleans traffic office to handle this unfortunate situation?

Mr. Douchebag is shooting me a mean look and keeps flexing his strained muscles. Is he trying to intimidate me? I feel sorry for Mr. Douchebag's shirt because the buttons are screaming at me. I'm also now getting a retired, worn-out porn star vibe from him. I'm not dogging porn stars. I love porn movies. I've seen my share of straight and gay porn, and he's one of the bad ones. Mr. Douchebag is as fake as his watch. He's intentionally showing it off to everyone who passes. Dude, just stop. It's fool's gold with cubic zirconium that you bought from a side street hustle. No one is impressed. Mr. Douchebag should be pissed at being stupid enough to spend money on that gumball designer watch. Not at me.

Mr. Douchebag: The ticket says it'll be $30. I'm not paying it. Now fix my ticket!

I'm impressed. I've never seen a piece of shit read before. Would you like an award? Should I be impressed that you've controlled your roid rage long enough not to punch me in the face? Would you like me to track down the parking meter officer? You can have a stern talk with her. I'd love to watch the five minutes of entertainment it would provide for me. Go drink a protein shake, and calm down before you pop out a hemorrhoid.

Me: I'm sorry, sir, I do not work for the City of New Orleans, and I cannot "fix" your ticket. Unfortunately, you obtained that ticket by illegally parking on a public street and not paying the meter within the allotted time frame. The hotel offers valet parking to protect you from receiving another parking violation. You parked on the street by your own choice, and thus you are responsible for your parking violation.

I sound like a robot. This typically happens when I'm being emotionless toward someone who hasn't earned my courtesy. This just pisses off Mr. Douchebag more. I love it. He doesn't like the fact that his magic man muscles are having no effect on me. I can see his neck muscles bulging, and his face is turning red. His Bolex is about to snap off his wrist. How much would it take of my calm demeanor and corporate way of talking to make someone slap the hell out of me? It's yet to happen, but I'm waiting for that day. Let's find out what Mr. Douchebag will do next.

Mr. Douchebag: You're being mean and uncooperative. I'm escaping from a hurricane! I will not pay for a valet. I will not pay for a parking ticket. You're the concierge here. This is your problem. You need to make a call and make it happen, or there'll be hell to pay!

I'm now figuratively rolling on the floor, laughing my ass off at everything wrong with that statement. Mr. Douchebag thinks I'm being mean? Are you going to start crying, little gorilla baby? Did I just pull your gross back hair on the school playground and kick dirt in your face? The poor little itty-bitty gorilla baby. You're escaping from a hurricane? So is everyone else staying here, and they aren't whining. We have a special low rate for hurricane evacuees, but Mr. Douchebag wants us to treat him like a celebrity. That shit ain't happening. We're doing everything we can to make sure our guests are having a great stay during this difficult situation. The hurricane came nowhere near Miami that year. The only hurricane is Hurricane Asshole who is standing in front of me right now. Mr. Douchebag's millionaire, cheap-as-fart ass is complaining about a $30 ticket that he straight up received all on his own. No. I will not call anyone for you. No, I can't fix your ticket. There is not a magic gay ticket-fixing concierge fairy at the New Orleans Police Department who will bend over for me and make it go away. You're a moron, and your breath smells like a juicy tuna fart.

Me: I understand your frustration. However, it's your choice to not valet with our hotel property. These are the current options I can offer you. If you decide to park with us, you will pay for valet charges per night per the rate displayed. If you decide to park on the public streets, they are metered and enforced. I'm sorry that you already received a ticket while in New Orleans. Parking restrictions and enforcement occur in every city. My suggestion is for you to move your vehicle to a legal parking spot and keep the meter paid in full to avoid receiving another parking violation.

I'm impressed with myself for staying so calm. He is nearly spitting at me, but he's starting to show signs of cracking. I'm guessing that his pea brain is slowly comprehending that he'll be paying that ticket. Just when I think I am getting through to him, his penis takes over. He now has an entirely different way of trying to get what he wants. Mr. Douchebag has a brilliant idea. He's going to pull a fast one on New Orleans and circumvent the parking restrictions. How does your head fit into your extremely tight, flower-patterned pants? I don't think he can cram his narrow fat head that far up his ass, but he does. It's not his lollipop taking up the room, so it must be his big muscles. Mr. Douchebag is such a colossal asshole. I'm just going to play the concierge game of answering with the most honest, professional answers I can. No, I'm not helping him with his ticket woes.

Mr. Douchebag: If I leave the ticket on the car, can you guarantee me that I won't get another ticket?

Me: I'm sorry, sir, but again I do not work for the City of New Orleans. I've seen multiple tickets on vehicles in the past. The outcome will always be in the city's favor. They have the right to ticket you, boot you, or tow your car away for multiple violations. You do not want your car towed in New Orleans. You're choosing to leave your vehicle parked illegally. You're choosing to leave a bright orange ticket displayed on your vehicle. Leaving it there does not guarantee you'll not receive another one. I will not make that guarantee to you.

I can't believe you'd think that would be okay. Granted, our police force is not the best in the nation, but they're smart enough to figure out what you're doing. They want to ticket your vehicle. Every dollar you spend on getting your car back pays their salaries. Did you just pull this idea out your giant asshole with both hands?

Mr. Douchebag: This is ridiculous. I want you to tell me that I can leave it there. I want you to guarantee me that I will not get another ticket. And I do not want the first ticket to show up on my driving record!

Me. I absolutely cannot guarantee that. Again, it's your choice to leave your vehicle parked in a space that you'll need to pay a meter for. This is your choice and neither I nor the hotel will be responsible for your actions in this matter. I highly suggest moving your vehicle if you wish to avoid another ticket. Your driving record is your personal business. I cannot help you with that. I can look up the number to your city's Department of Motor Vehicles, if you choose to speak to someone about your driving record. I'm here to help.

You know what I want? I want you to walk away before I kick you in your tiny dick. We don't always get what we want. To be honest, we rarely get what we want. I'm at a loss. How the hell do you expect me to guarantee you something like that? Are you from the land of impossible assholes? I know your momma didn't raise you to be the turd you are. I want to meet the woman who gave birth to you and then shove you back in until you're fully cooked. Your mother would and should be ashamed of you. You're an embarrassment to assholes everywhere. My vote is to kick you out of the Asshole League of America.

Mr. Douchebag: I want to speak with a manager right now!

Manager: How may I help you, sir?

I know what the manager is going to say. The "word porn" is like rock music to my ears. The manager on duty repeats everything that I said to Mr. Douchebag but does it with less panache. I'm impressed. I respect hotel managers as much as I respect my parents. I never want to be a hotel manager. They have one of the hardest jobs in the hotel industry, ranked right up there with front desk agents. The main difference between a hotel manager and a hotel front desk agent is that everyone shits on a manager, from the guests to the employees. Everyone.

Mr. Douchebag: Fart this shit. I can't believe none of you can take care of this for me. I'm going to leave my car there, and it better not get ticketed again. You'll be hearing from my lawyer.

Mr. Douchebag walks away and toward his shiny BMW. He's shaking his fist and rattling his cheap Bolex in the air. I feel sorry for the entire city of Miami. I hope someone beats your ass, steals your cheap watch, and drives away in your BMW. I doubt that'll happen because no one wants to get asshole on their hands.

Me: Have a nice day, and enjoy our lovely city.

Choice. Life is about the choices we make. I mention this to guests often not to be an asshole, but to give guests options. Please choose wisely, and don't be that next asshole I write about. It's fun to dish about the guests. Without assholes, I wouldn't have good stories to write about. However, I don't come to your job and treat you like an asshole, so don't come to mine and treat me like one. The funny thing about this story is what happened after Mr. Miami Douchebag left my desk. I had just worked a twelve-hour shift, which is not uncommon for a concierge. Just for shits and giggles, I decided to walk the long way around the building. I wanted to look at Mr. Miami Douchebag's BMW window and see what I knew in my heart would be there. Karma has a love affair with hospitality workers in New Orleans. She loves us, she really does. I approached the BMW, and like two bright orange stars in heaven, there was a second ticket on Mr. Miami Douchebag's window. My heart leaped with immense joy.

I didn't contact my very good friend who's a meter maid in downtown New Orleans. I didn't talk to a very kind lady who comes in daily for a bottle of water and to say hello. I didn't make a small request. Dominique would never print a ticket after a lengthy afternoon conversation with a kind concierge to make him feel better. That would just be unethical. I wish I had been there when Mr. Miami Douchebag saw he was ticketed twice. He's now paying twice as much for parking, plus I hope they both go on his driving record. No, we never heard from his lawyer. People who threaten a lawsuit typically have no intention of following through on it because they know they're in the wrong. Mr. Miami Douchebag was full of shit, and his empty threat was just that, empty. No, he didn't complain about the second ticket. He tucked his gorilla nuts between his legs and ran back to his state. Good riddance to bad rubbish. I picture him driving back to Miami, upset that the little concierge twerp had been right. He should have paid the meter or valet-serviced his vehicle. The fact that he had to pay both of those tickets brings joy to my soul. Karma kicked him in the nuts, and I gave her a high five. The moral of this story is very clear and easy to comprehend. Choose to be a better person, admit your mistakes, and don't be an asshole to a concierge.

LIMOUSINE LINDA

It's not always hotel guests who cause a ruckus at the concierge desk. There are occasions when members of the general public come inside the hotel to rear their ugly heads. These people walk in thinking they own the world. They merely exist to show how gross people can be. For me, the epitome of that kind of person was Limousine Linda. It was a sunny afternoon and the lobby was packed with tourists ready to venture out and experience all that New Orleans had to offer. New Orleans has a festival every weekend, and this weekend was no different. I was answering questions, giving out maps, talking about festivals, and pretending to be the perfectly charming Southern man that I am.

Limousine Linda, a.k.a. Satan herself, strolls in through the front door and, like an anorexic bull in a china cabinet, crashes through my day. She practically throws her overnight whore bag at me. Various gross items spill out and onto my desk. I don't assist in picking up her many whore-shaded red lipsticks, used panties, or the roll of quarters that falls out, wrapped in a dirty sock. Images of classic women's prison movie scenes flash in my mind. Linda is super white, paper thin, with a sunken face. If you thumped her hard, she'd bruise. Her cheekbones are protruding outward in an unnatural way. Linda earns her living by sucking golf balls through a garden hose. I bite my lip and smile. I'm waiting to hear what or who pissed her off. She's mad at either valet services or one of the bellmen. Who screwed up now, and why are you mad at me?

Linda: I don't understand what the hell is happening! The limousine my dumbass assistant scheduled is not here! I need to get picked up, and I need to get picked up now! This is unprofessional!

Me: I'm very sorry for the problem with your scheduled limousine pickup. I don't see information on any transportation booked today through Concierge Services. I apologize. We do our very best to keep a record of all our scheduled departures. Do you have the name and a contact number for your chosen limousine service? I'll call the representative and help figure out where the breakdown in communication was. I'd also be happy to call your room if you'd like to relax while you wait.

She grabs her items from my desk and throws them in her bag. She simultaneously knocks my concierge sign and a stack of papers off my desk. She smiles sideways, looks down at the mess, and makes no effort to pick up the clutter she caused. I collect the items with a smile, blinking my eyes in that nice, hateful way. I hate people who think they should treat me like a servant just because I'm on the clock and they aren't. She was purposely trying to start a fight with me from the minute she walked in. I will not cuss, I will not call her names . . . not yet.

Linda: Ugh, I'm not a guest at . . . this place. I've been waiting outside for forty-five Goddamn minutes, and I need to know where my farting driver is! My dumbass assistant scheduled this damn pickup months ago. She's getting fired for this! My plane leaves in an hour.

Hold up! Now I want to cuss you out. You farting, rail-thin, evil stepmother. Take that thick broom lodged up your ass and stroll out my doorway. First, you sound like a goat giving birth, so calm your shit down. Second, you're not even a guest at my hotel, and you're cussing and raising hell in my lobby? What about my face tells you that I give a shit about a limousine pickup that your assistant set up for you? I didn't set it up, and I could care less where you're going. Your flight is in an hour? You're not making that flight, sweetie. I'm sure your witch's broom can express-fly you home, along with your flying monkeys. Look here, Linda, things are about to get a whole lot more interesting because now I don't have to be nice to you. You're not my guest. You're a rude lady who slithered in from outside just to make someone else feel bad.

Me: I would appreciate you not cussing in this very public area. There are small children present. I would prefer not to expose them to your language. Although you're NOT a guest with us, New Orleans loves all its visitors. Can you please provide me with a confirmation number and a phone number?

Linda: Here's the phone number. Hurry up!

Linda, you're really testing my patience. I don't have to place this call for you. I could tell you to go fart yourself and figure it out on your own. Call your assistant and have her figure it out. She gets paid to put up with your abuse. I'm secretly hoping she screwed you out of a ride to miss your flight. She needs the extra day off from you. I dislike you based sheerly on the way you're speaking to me about her. I can't imagine how she feels about you. You get respect when you give respect, and so far, you're failing. I call the number she provided, and Shaneese answers the phone.

Shaneese: This is Shaneese, hows can I helps cho today? Ummmmhmmmmm, gurl.

Me: Hello, I have a lady here who is NOT a guest at my hotel. She has a limousine scheduled for pickup, and the driver has not arrived. Can you please help me with this? Correct. She's trying to locate her limousine. Yes, her name is Linda. No. She doesn't know her confirmation number. I understand. You don't say, Shaneese? Really? Let me just tell Linda what you said. One moment, please.

Shaneese is an awesome-sounding young black woman. She's direct and powerful. I love it. I speak New Orleans sassy black woman dialect. It's an art form. We're becoming best friends very fast. I don't put Shaneese on hold because I want her to hear everything that is being said. I've learned that phone representatives are more willing to help you out if they're not put on hold. They like to hear the juice, too. I am about to have a lot of fun with the information I've just been given.

Me: Ma'am, where do you think you're supposed to be getting picked up from?

Linda: What the hell does that matter? I just got off the cruise ship! Why? Let me have the phone! I'll take care of this damn problem myself!

I hear Shaneese do that "Oohhh, hell no" and smack her lips. She's preparing for a knock-out, drag-down fight with Linda. She has nothing to worry about. I got your back, Shaneese. I'm not handing the phone over to Linda. She may stank it up with her bad attitude. I'd never do that to Shaneese. That's called a guest ambush. Don't pass that on to another hospitality worker. It's a shitty move.

Me: Please stop yelling at me and lower your voice. Let me get this crystal clear. You walked a mile from the cruise terminal to my hotel. Why? Did you honestly expect that your limousine driver knows you're here?

Linda: It's disgusting at that damn terminal. I was not going to stay there like a common person, waiting on my driver to pick me up. Give me the damn phone!

Is there a reason you like to use the word **damn** so much? What the fart do you mean by saying "like a common person"? You're not the queen of anything, unless it's the queen of mean. I'm surprised Linda walked over here without stepping on people all the way down the street. I doubt that in the real world, she's carried around on a golden throne. The only things golden in her life are those golden showers she loves. I don't see muscular, well-toned, oiled-up men feeding her grapes, while cooling her with giant feather fans. The Queen of Sheba she is not.

Me: No, ma'am. There's no need for you to speak with the representative. I can handle whatever needs to be done to take care of this situation.

Linda starts cussing at me again and wants to speak to Shaneese. She's acting like a damn fool. Hell has no fury like a woman denied a phone. I'm holding onto the phone like it's the Holy Grail. Over my cold dead body will Linda get this phone receiver out of my hand. There's no chance in hell I'm going to expose someone else to her wrath. She's screaming at me like an old crow on a chain-link fence. I don't get many chances to be firm with a guest. Linda is probably used to getting her way. Not this time. I always strive to be professional with people, brutally honest, and resist the urge to punch them in the face. My limits are being tested. I cock my head, loosen my tongue, and pull up my big boy concierge pants. Let the fires of hell rain down!

Me: I'm going to tell you this just once more. Stop yelling at me. Raise your voice at me again, and this conversation is over. I'm not sorry if it sounds rude, but I need for you to hear me clearly. I need you to collect yourself, or I'll call security. I'll have you removed from the property, and it'll be embarrassing for you. This is your final warning about your abusive language, and you'll not be getting another. Your use of profanity is unwarranted and uncalled for in the presence of small children. I also don't appreciate it. You're not a guest here. You left your cruise ship to come here. You left your pickup location that your assistant set up for you. You knew where and when you needed to be there. You missed it. Please feel free to talk to my manager if you don't like what I've said or how I said it. Shaneese said your driver has been waiting for over an hour. He has attempted to call you multiple times with no answer.

Linda: I don't answer my phone if I don't recognize the number.

Me: I'm not done. Shaneese is willing to redirect the driver to come pick you up here, which is very nice of her. She doesn't have to and is not required to. She's also not going to charge you the extra pickup fee, which is extremely nice of her. I think that's fair since you left the terminal. Otherwise, she'll redirect your pickup to someone else, and you'll be catching a cab on the curb with the rest of the common people leaving the city. What should I tell her?

Shaneese is laughing loud enough that Linda can hear her through the phone. Linda blinks like an old possum trapped in headlights. It's this moment that you see reality set in. She has an "Oh, shit" expression plastered across her face. Do you know what happens next? Linda gets real nice, real quick and surprises me by saying a kind word.

Linda: Please ask her to pick me up. I'm stressed because I don't want to miss my flight.

She looks defeated. Mission accomplished. I just spanked that ass without even paying the cover charge for it. Before I can relay this to Shaneese, she says, "Done, please stay on dis phone until after da guest be leaving your earshot, honey."

Me: The driver is being redirected to our location. Please see yourself to the curb, and he'll pick you up in just a few minutes. Have a nice day and a safe flight away. Goodbye.

I rarely ever end a conversation with a pointed ending. **Goodbye** to me is final, and there is no coming back from it. When I say goodbye, it's like I just threw you out of a moving vehicle. Linda is not even worth pumping the brakes for. She does qualify for an extra hard push to enjoy the asphalt meal.

Linda: Okay.

All I get is an "okay"? Why is saying thank you so hard for some people? I didn't have to make that phone call. Shaneese didn't have to break her company's policy. Linda could have at least had the decency to fake a thank you. She grabs her overnight whore bag and slowly walks out the door. For someone in a hurry, it sure doesn't look like she's in a rush. I hope she gets a heel stuck in the bricks and shatters both her hips. Wait. That's evil. Screw it, I'll pray on it later. I hear a giggle, then the voice of Shaneese.

Shaneese: Gurl, thank you for that. I was not gonna be helping dat lady. She sounded mean, and she missed her ride, but I got cho, gurl, I got cho. If you needs something again, you just ax for me. Thank you.

Shaneese ends her sentence with another loud lip smack and an audible head roll. I'm not making fun of the way she was talking. I'm reveling in it. It reminds me of my hometown girlfriends. It's funny when people think I'm a woman on the phone, and it's never bothered me in the least. I have a soft voice and missed my calling at being a top-notch phone sex operator. I'd be a millionaire by now. It works to my advantage until Bulging Bubba arrives and realizes he was flirting with a dude over the phone. It's okay, Bulging Bubba. I enjoyed the call, too.

Me: I got cho, too, gurl. Have a good day.

*

Your greatest ally can be the random stranger on the other end of the phone. That person is working hard, too. Why not work together to make everyone's job easier? The last thing people need is Satan yelling at them for a mistake the guest rightfully made on her own. People at call centers are faceless. They're talked to like they're not people. Guess what? They're people with real feelings, and they should be respected as if they are standing in front of you. I'm not saying they're all angels. I have dealt with some dumb-ass phone agents, but I still try my best to respect them. I have taken a stand many times against handing a phone over to a guest. Limousine Linda was no different but super nastier. You want to yell at somebody, then yell at me. I'm right here looking you in the face, and I won't back down from you.

FOUR BLIND SOUTHERN MEANIES

I deal with people of every color and degree of candor daily. I'm rarely surprised by people. However, there are times when even the nicest-looking old ladies surprise me with their ignorance and racist comments. Southern women are the best at covering up what they want to openly say. They have mastered the art of the backhanded compliment. I was graced with four old ladies from Virginia who were far from being good Southern belles. I've never wanted to kick four old broads in the crotch as much as I wanted to squarely kick each of them. I imagine the air would fill with a cloud of crotch smog. It would puff out from their dusty, cobweb-covered nether regions, and you'd never get it out of your clothes. Please don't kick old ladies in the crotch. It's downright mean and just plain nasty. No matter how nasty they are, just breathe, compose yourself, and cock your foot back in place.

I was completely happy listening to these meanies being mean to one another from a safe distance. It was only a few moments later that they decided to include me in their conversation. It was an interesting dance from there on out. These four Southern meanies were blind to the fact that the world had changed. You don't talk to people that way in today's age. We, as a society, will never grow into a better world unless we change our outdated views of the world. We should not adopt and carry forward the way people have been mistreated in the past, but instead pave a way to love and acceptance, or the future generation will fail.

Carol: Hey, Betty Ann. Don't you look healthy in that dress! It fits you so snug. I bet you have to just peel it off you, don't you?

Betty Ann: Thank you. Would you just look at how beautiful you are after all this time? Your dress goes so well with your plain skin tone. I just love how it hangs off your body.

Wow! I can't believe these ladies are friends. They don't own nail files because they sharpen their claws on one another's comments. Yes, Carol, I agree. Betty Ann's dress is way too tight. It doesn't look flattering on her, but damn, you just called her fat, and she knows you did. That's about the meanest thing you could say to a friend who has put on a few pounds. It was funny as hell, though, and I'm glad Betty Ann didn't miss a beat. She just called Carol old and flabby. Yes, Betty Ann, I agree that she has more skin hanging off her body than a shar-pei puppy. Do you want to enter a cage and fight it out? I'll pay good money to see two old broads smack down in a death match. I am quite happy sitting here with my hands under my chin, my eyes open wide, and sporting a big grin. Every time they speak, I perk up to hear the response. Maybe that's why they take notice of me hanging on every word. Damn it, Ren!

Dixie: You two are just so funny. I wish you had husbands to hear how you talk. My husband is amazing, rich, and handsome.

Edie: I'm not going to say a word.

Wow, Dixie! You just called them old spinsters with no men in their lives. You're pure, unfiltered evil. You not only told them they were unloved and unwanted, but you rubbed it in their faces that you have a husband and they don't. Edie was the one I was indifferent about. I guess if you have nothing nice to say, then don't say anything at all, or tell Edie. She agreed with everything they said. She just nodded her head and giggled like she was already two sheets in the wind or high on life. Go ahead, girl, stick your head in the ground and pretend you're not here.

Carol: How do these four silver foxes look to you, boy?

Me: Good morning. You all look very lovely. If you need any assistance, Concierge Services is here to help.

Did I hear you correctly? Did you honestly just call me "boy"? I'm not your boy, and this is not the Old South. I'm a grown-ass man with huge balls. We discussed this earlier in the book if you skipped that part. Yes, I'm offended as hell by the way you just said that. You didn't squeeze me out of that lump you're hiding under your mom jeans. By the way, they went out of fashion thirty years ago. I don't think any man would like to be called "boy," especially not by four "silver foxes." I shot the last silver fox that crossed my path and ate her in a stew with a nice red wine. Correct me if I'm wrong, but I thought the term **silver fox** was used to describe older men. I noticed the mustache and chin hairs you're sporting, so you could be a man. Kudos to your tucking skills. They're spot on.

Dixie: We're going to tear this city up! We'd like to start with the real side of New Orleans. Do you understand what I mean, boy? You know, we're from Virginia, and they're taking down all our

Confederate monuments. It's a crime to be tearing all those down. They've been up since my daddy was young. What do you think about "those people" tearing them down?

Carol: You have that right, Dixie. "Those people" are never happy with just letting things be. It's our history.

I already guessed where you ladies were from by your first two underhanded comments about race. Here's one more thing I dislike. I hate when people skirt around what they really want to say. By "those people," do you mean black people? The people who care for me and feed me, the community of people that I live with and that I was basically raised in? I want to punch Carol and Dixie in their smug faces. I was raised in the South; I get it. I knew ladies like these growing up, but I didn't think they still existed. I understand that the generation before us was raised in a different atmosphere, but that's no excuse. You've had three hundred years to know better, to be better. You may not be breaking the rules, but you're bending the hell out of them. The one rule I've always followed is never talk about politics, race, or religion with a guest. This is a golden rule in the service industry.

Me: I don't really follow politics. I can suggest some lovely tours of the French Quarter or the historic Garden District. They're full of rich, fascinating history.

Betty Ann: You should really follow what's happening in current events. A good concierge would know what's happening in the world around him.

It's not that I don't follow current events, it's that I don't want to discuss them with you. You don't want to know about current events anyway, only the history you want to hear about. Thanks for being a camel toe about it. I don't need you telling me what I should be following. I'm physically holding down my eyebrow from raising.

Dixie: I'd love to see the old houses of the Garden District. That's where all the real people of New Orleans lived back in the good ole days of the mighty South.

Me: What brings you ladies to New Orleans?

It's not that I care, but I'm desperate to change the subject. The four blind Southern meanies are here on vacation and staying with us before their cruise sets sail. They're riding a steamboat up the Mississippi River from here to Saint Louis. The journey is meant to be a lovely weeklong ride, stopping at various points to learn the history of our country. I've never seen anyone younger than eighty going on this tour. For all I know, Charon is the boat captain taking souls across the River Styx. These ladies make it very clear that they're only interested in visiting the old plantation homes. I'm guessing they want to relive the glory days when they owned servants and treated people like utter dirt. That's just a guess, though. You can hide behind your nice old lady exterior and sly comments, but you're not fooling anyone.

Carol: I heard about the Garden District. It's supposed to be amazing. Yes, book that Garden District walking tour for us, boy.

Edie: Yes.

Dixie: Are you ladies sure you can walk that far without help? Maybe we should get ya'll scooters with cup holders for our mint juleps.

Me: It'll be my pleasure to assist. Please give me a moment to take care of this tour booking with a phone representative. I'll give you directions to your start point and a Garden District map to help you find your way.

Sweet Baby Jesus eating ice cream! You just called me "boy" again. Rude! Does it look like I want to dance for your Virginia nickels? Dixie is one shady Southern belle. There is not one time when she opens her mouth that she doesn't have something pointed to say to her friends or to me. I'm getting mad right now just writing about this. Dixie basically said they're too frail to walk. I hope her friends rent heavy, high-powered scooters with rotating spikes on the wheels. I can watch them take turns running Dixie's ass over and over again. I make the walking tour reservation for them with a big grimace. I am done with the four blind meanies, but little do I know that I will get one more chance to feel the sting of their comments the next day.

Carol: Good morning.

Me: Good morning, ladies.

Carol: How are you doing this fine morning?

Did someone drink the nice juice this morning? Maybe yesterday was just in my imagination? Wait. What's wrong with me? I'm now making excuses for these mean Southern ladies who hate black people and kiss the toes of Confederate monuments. Maybe they were tired from a long flight? Maybe they were just being cranky? Maybe I was hearing them wrong? Was I creating a dialogue in my head that really wasn't there? I do that often.

Dixie: Just to let you know, we're very upset with the tour you sent us on. The Garden District was lovely, and the houses were exactly like I pictured them, but the tour guide was less than to be desired. I just don't think people like that should be allowed to give that tour. A tour guide like that can only truly understand one side of history, and it was not the side we cared to hear anything about. At least, she knew about the houses and gardens.

Edie: Yes, I agree.

Betty Ann: I was appalled, but I made the most out of the unfortunate situation. I only wanted to hear about what we paid for.

Carol: I was going to ask for a refund, but I have a heart. I understand people like that are on welfare and have at least a dozen kids to feed. Although it sickens me that my tax dollars are paying for her to get pregnant every year.

Damn it! You all fooled me. Betty Ann and Edie may not say much, but they threw in their racist two cents. I should have known you didn't mean good morning, you meant "Good morning" as an opening to complain to me. Dixie is the devil, and the gang got one over on the poor "boy" at the desk. Carol can go fart herself in every direction I can think of and a few that probably haven't been invented yet. It's time to turn on my own Southern charm.

Me: I'm sorry. Did they not have a trained historian as a tour guide? Did she not tell you the history of New Orleans? Did she not explain the houses, culture, and people of New Orleans? We are a three-hundred-year-old city, and there's a lot of history to cover.

Carol: Yes, she did all that. But she can't really know.

Me: How did she not really know? The tour company I suggested does an amazing job of explaining to you what the history of New Orleans was from everyone's viewpoint. I understand that you can look at history in different ways, but, overall, it's history. The facts are the facts. History is written by the victors, but it may not always accurately depict the real history from all sides. Do you feel she was making up stories that are not true? I'm sorry, but I don't understand your complaint. I would love to give the tour company feedback on your experience. Can you explain more?

I can be defensive about my suggestions, and it gets the better of me, but I'm done with this conversation. I know exactly what she's implying. Two can play this game. I'm just a stupid "boy" who doesn't get their hints. They're going to have to lay it out for me like I'm a child. I'm clueless to the cryptic racism. I'm going to keep digging into all four of these blind Southern meanies until one of them says the word

black. Please, please, say it, so I can breathe a sigh of relief. I want confirmation that I'm right, and you're all terrible ladies. That's not fair of me to generalize all of them. Edie was just following the pack mentality. I'm sure they have families, friends, and many lovely qualities but routinely suppress them with hate.

Dixie: I just feel that a colored person can't understand what it's like to live in one of those white-owned private houses.

And there it is. Dixie just laid it all out for me. The three other ladies all take a sip of their lemon sweet tea while fanning themselves. They also take a group inhalation at the exact same time, collectively breathing in the racist stank. Oh, please! It's not like all you ladies weren't thinking it. Dixie just grew a pair of lady balls and said it. She not only said "colored" but emphasized that all the houses were white-owned homes. I have a reality check for you, darling. They're beautiful on the outside and can be gross on the inside. A good portion of those beautiful homes on Saint Charles Avenue are apartments and not all white-owned. They have shifted hands so many times that the owner could be anyone. I sent you there to learn, not to judge the tour guide on the color of her skin. I'm not sorry that you had to learn from an African American woman. I was secretly hoping she would be your tour guide. She's amazing and one of the best tour guides in the city.

Me: I'll give the tour company your feedback.

Dixie: Please do that, boy. Thanks.

Again? Boy? I wish I could slap my "boy" across your face. Dixie then proceeds to wait and stare at me. I hope you aren't waiting for an apology, Dixie. It'll be a cold day in hell before that happens. She stares at me. She is waiting for me to offer her something. Dixie and her mindless posse can move along. The only thing I will offer her is a shart in a cup. I'm done playing their card game of Racist Bridge. Are you proud of yourself? You said the word **colored**. You do not get a cookie. You do not get a mint julep for passing go. What you do get is a mental kick in the crotch. Can you tell yet that I enjoy giving a good kick in the crotch?

Me: Have a nice day, and enjoy our lovely city.

Edie: Yes.

*

I do not give the tour company the feedback. It would serve no purpose but to make one hard-working tour guide feel bad about herself. I have no problem giving negative or positive feedback to tour companies, but I will not give hurtful feedback. I wrote this story to show that not everything in the hotel industry is funny; it can be downright awful. Sometimes the situation is just wrong on many levels. There are still people who want to squash other people because of their race, religion, or sexual orientation. I've experienced it all, and it's given me a tougher skin. It has marked my soul. I'm a little more hesitant to express my honest self to people. I'm more aware that a conversation can turn around on you in the matter of one sentence. People say hospitality workers are jaded; it's because that constant slap on the face hurts. People like these four blind Southern meanies change you. Being talked down to, time and time again, wears down the soul. I love talking to older people who have decades of life experience on me. The way we learn is from the people who came before us. However, the four blind Southern meanies are people you don't want to learn from. The reason I stay in the hospitality industry is for that next guest who makes my job rewarding. These are the people who remind me that good people still exist in this harsh world. They're the diamonds that shine bright in a dark field of hotel guests. They make it all worth my time.

LADY BEVERLY OF AWESOMESHIRE

It was a typical day like any other. There was nothing special going on in the city. I may have talked to three people all day. I wanted to go home, eat chips, and fall asleep on the couch with our dogs.

I'm looking down, reading a book, when an elderly lady pushing eighty sits down at my desk. Lady Beverly of Awesomeshire is a Valkyrie, and she's a fierce, silent warrior. How do older ladies move so quietly? I almost don't look up until I hear an abrupt little cough. It's politer to cough than say something rude to get my attention. I do a quick scan of her. I'm usually excellent at reading people before they even speak. She has a definite grandma vibe with a pinched face and many, many wrinkles. Her hands look rough, and her body is still very shapely for someone of her advanced age. Beverly's clothes look as old as she does. I imagine in her glory days she would've been considered fashionable, but now her clothes are dated, to match her overall appearance.

My first instinct is that this will be my typical conversation. She will ask where to eat, what to do, blah, blah, blah. I'll be cute with a big smile, feigning interest as she rambles on about her grandchild's graduation, daughter's upcoming marriage, or some other milestone moment that has nothing to do with me. I love listening to grandma stories, but after years of hearing them, they all start to sound the same. I am in for the biggest surprise of my life.

Beverly: Hello, dear. My name is Beverly. Most people call me Bev. How are you today?

Me: Hello, Ms. Beverly. My name is Ren. My day is going well, just your typical day in New Orleans. How may I assist you?

Beverly: Young man, I was just wondering if you could tell me where's a good place to have a nice drink?

Here we go. This lady is going to get my standard answers. She called me "young man." That's cute. I don't know this random lady sitting in front of me. I'll not be calling her Bev. In my mind, she'll always be Lady Beverly, but out of respect, Ms. Beverly it shall be. How do I know this is not a test by an undercover agent? Yes, we have those in the hotel world. I'm not dropping my guard for a sweet old lady. I'm going to send her to the same bars as everyone else because they're close, safe, and reasonably priced.

Me: There's a lovely bar just a few blocks away. It's a nice place to have a drink alone or with friends. I would highly recommend it, Ms. Beverly.

My smile must have given me away because Lady Beverly is not having my standard answer. She lets me know this very quickly. She leans forward, lowers her voice, and clenches her hands together. Lady Beverly, you're awesome.

Beverly: What kind of bullshit answer is that, kiddo? I was born and raised here. I may be older than dirt now, but I was a street rat back in my day. I know there are better bars in this damn dirty city than the piece of shit one you just suggested. You seem like a smart sport, so try again. I've been sitting in the lobby for the last hour listening to you talk. You run a good game, but I know you've got more up your sleeve than that crap.

Oh, hell. You've been listening to me? Where were you hiding? You are a silent warrior! Grandma Warrior will be the name of my next play, and I'll dedicate it to you. Lady Beverly curses so much that I can't put it in this book, or it will be X-rated. Beverly can make sailors blush. Is there anything better than a proper old lady who cusses long and hard? I have so much mad respect for Lady Beverly. Plus, I love being called **kiddo**, **sport**, **pal**, or any other dated term when it's genuinely used as a term of endearment. Ten points go to Lady Beverly. I am wrong for judging her. She puts me in my place, and I deserve it. I want to know her story. Everyone else in this lobby can go to hell. You have the stage, Lady Beverly, and I'm your adoring captive audience.

Me: I . . . ummm. Let's get a feel for exactly what you want to get out of your New Orleans vacation. Can you please give me an idea of the bars you typically like to experience?

I'm sweating so much that beads of perspiration are forming on my forehead, and my back feels like Niagara Falls. I'm nervous talking to this old lady. How did this happen? I'm always in control of the conversation. Has she placed a voodoo spell on me? I can't handle another hex this year. Please stop wrinkling your nose, crossing your arms, or silently chanting under your breath. Her vibe totally changes in the time it takes you to snap your fingers.

Beverly: First, stop treating me like I'm fragile. I'm tough as nails. Second, stop talking slow and loud to me. I can hear everything. I'm old, not ancient. I can carry a conversation without forgetting what I just said. Think of me like a friend you haven't seen in years. Impress me. And I must insist that you call me Bev; none of that proper concierge shit you're trained to do. Not Beverly or Ms. Beverly, but Bev and only Bev.

Me: I'm sorry, Ms. Beverly—I mean, Bev.

Beverly: Don't be sorry, be better.

You're not a lady. I love it. I've changed my mind. Bev, it is. What the hell did I do to you, lady? I'm being punished just for opening my mouth. Normally, this would piss me off, but the way she says it makes me sit up and take notice. She has this vibrant power to her. The way she speaks is commanding, and I am not going to disappoint her. What do you do as a concierge when placed in this position? You take a chance and become informal as hell. Bev requested it, and after all, I must do as the guest requests. What's the worst thing that can happen? Secret shoppers don't cuss like Bev does. My employer could write me up for talking to a guest inappropriately, but Bev opened the door, and I'm going to run through it. I lean forward and loosen my lips. I also lower my voice, just in case there are other warriors lurking around, listening to our conversation.

Me: Do you want a dirty dive bar with whores, pimps, and gigolos? You know, the kind of shady bar where your feet stick to the floor, the bathroom has glory holes, drug deals are going down, people are snorting coke off the backs of toilet tanks, and there's a constant thump of disco music in the background. Is that your speed? I can also send you to an upscale joint. A place that's too fancy for the way you talk, the drinks are overpriced, the food pretends to be five-star, but it's dollar-store turds wrapped in parchment, and the servers only care about how much green you're going to drop on them. They'll kiss your ass and not wipe their mouths after. It's fake as shit, but your money will spend. You have money, but you don't like to show it. Am I right? I get a feeling that you can change what you say and how you say it about as fast as I do. You fit in anywhere, and I like that. My suggestion, go to a soul food kitchen place with live music. The food is so good, you'll want to kick your neighbor's cat; the drinks will knock you on your backside; the music is unreal; and you can dance your gams off. I bet all the guys there will give you a look like you're the only backseat Betty in the joint.

I use every colloquialism in my vocabulary. I make my own head hurt and take a chance that she won't backhand me for it. You want the real me, Bev? You're getting it in spades. I may get burned for talking to a guest this way, but I love a good challenge.

Beverly: That's the New Orleans I remember and love. Tell me about the first place and the last place. People are assholes, but I know how to swim upriver in shit. Give me the details, and make it good.

Seriously? The way I talked to you just worked? I'm sitting here in shock that she didn't get offended. I'm ready for her to pull out a ruler and slap my hands red, but instead she pulls out a sword and smiles. Her eyes are on fire, her hands have relaxed, and her voice has changed to more of a controlled giggle. The stern warnings have ceased, and I can feel her soul is searching my face for more information. I'm quickly falling in mad, deep love with Bev.

Me: I've a feeling we're going to be great friends, Bev.

Beverly: I have the same feeling, Sherlock.

Beverly stayed with us for five days. I know more about her fascinating life than I do about some of my best friends. She was born to a poor family and grew up in Algiers Point. It was not the nice part of Algiers Point in those days. She made it very clear that it was the dangerous, working-class section. There are remnants of her neighborhood remaining today, but for the most part, it's long forgotten. Beverly's mother had a singing voice that belonged on Broadway but was stuck in New Orleans. She would sing at home, in church, or anywhere with an audience, but it didn't pay the bills. Her mother cleaned houses, washed clothes, cooked, and did other odd jobs to help put food on the table. Every cent she earned helped support the family. Her mom was always in poor health, and Beverly was required to work when her mother couldn't. Her mother was limited by what she could do because of her illness. She fought and won many rounds with cancer. Her mother didn't consider her children to be her priority. Her mother's priority was providing for her father when he came home from a long day at work. She was, sadly, a maid in and out of the home. Beverly doesn't remember a time when there wasn't a cold beer and a hot meal waiting for him on the table when he got home. She spoke of her mom with painful affection. I could tell she missed her greatly because her voice broke, and she was holding back tears. She had to pause and catch her breath several times. It made my heart sink. She loved her mother, and this was just the way it was in those days. Beverly was not living in New Orleans when her mother lost the last battle she waged. She looked off in the distance when she told me she'd missed her mother's funeral. Yet missing her mother's funeral was not her greatest regret in life. Her greatest regret was not telling her mom every day that she was a priority in Beverly's life, and that Beverly loved her more than words could describe.

Beverly's father was a blue-collar factory worker to his core. He worked hard to provide what little he could for his family, and all he did was work. Every day, all day, routinely without complaint, he worked. Beverly was not a daddy's girl, but she tugged on his coattails often. He taught her to be strong and independent. He treated her mother and her well but wasn't overly affectionate. She gave him credit for creating the person she is today. He died four months after her mother. She was unable to come home for her father's funeral either. However, she had a long talk with him before his death and felt she had closure. It was as if she had his blessing not to be there.

Beverly was convinced that he'd died of a broken heart . . . or starvation. She was joking about the latter because her mother wasn't there to cook him a good meal every night. She had one older brother. His name was Harold. He died when she was a teenager, before she left home. She didn't say much about him, except there was an accident and he didn't come home. I got the feeling it was something she didn't like to talk about, and I didn't push the subject. Heartache doesn't dull over time; it just scars over. I felt this was one of Beverly's more painful scars.

Beverly was a smart girl in school but nothing that would propel her far in life. Her father didn't have the money to give her a proper education, and she only attended school when she wanted to. She bartended on Bourbon Street, worked in restaurants, stripped in clubs for cash, and did a few other things. She was not ashamed of what she did for money but would never wish that life on a young girl. I got the feeling she turned tricks a few times, but again I wasn't going to pry. You do things in life to survive, and that's okay. Beverly was very mature for her age, and she could pass for much older. The bars never asked her age, and she never told them. She was almost eighteen when she met her husband in a strip club. His name was Jacob. From the way she described him, he was several years, if not more, older than her. He had a very old soul but was extremely youthful. Her exact words were: "He's older, but not in that gross way, you know?" This made me laugh out loud. He waited until she was eighteen and made sure she graduated from high school before he would marry her. That just made her love him more.

Jacob took her away from New Orleans when she was twenty because he landed a high-paying job in Detroit. That job turned into another high-paying job in San Francisco, which turned into an even-higher paying job on Wall Street in New York City. Jacob was extremely successful. I was right. They were not rich. To say they were rich would be an understatement; they were wealthy beyond measure.

I asked why she was staying with us. I'm not knocking my hotel, but we're not the queen's palace. It's certainly not up to the level of her wealth. I'm also not the professional ass-kissing concierge she's probably used to. She said that although she had all the money she could ever want, she was still that small girl born to a factory worker and a woman who was treated like a maid. Beverly never forgot where she came from and was proud of that. Status and wealth in life don't make the person, and she never wanted to be defined by them. Beverly said she'd give all her fortune away in a second if this could bring back those she had loved and lost. She was grateful to have money and happy to give it to others. I wanted to know everything! I got exactly what I wanted with a smile and some tears for good measure.

Beverly had done everything, and I don't mean that as an overexaggeration. Jacob loved and trusted her very much. He gave her free rein to do whatever she wanted. She could stay at home and be a socialite, or she could work. The choice was hers to make. She chose to work for nonprofits across the country. She went to college late in life and earned a degree in social work. The list of her accomplishments seemed endless. A life well spent. She marched for equality for women and gay rights. She gave her time to numerous charities. She worked for battered women's organizations and started an educational program for children in low-income families. She routinely visited gay bars to pass out information on safe sex and openly supported HIV clinics. She provided aid to those who didn't have a hot meal and took people to shelters on cold nights. She was a hero to people who had no champion, yet she never considered herself a hero.

Beverly sounds like a saint, doesn't she? There are many types of people in this world, and even the kindest people struggle with demons on their shoulders. Beverly was no different, and she was far from being a saint. She admitted to cheating on Jacob once with a man she worked with. Lust was her deadly sin.

I asked her, "Why jeopardize everything for one night of sex?" She said it just happened. People are animals with carnal desires that are too powerful to resist. She was young, and it was hard to imagine that she was going to be with one person the rest of her life. She knew it was wrong the second after the deed was done. It was the hardest discussion with Jacob she'd ever have during their long life together. He shook his head, then hugged her and never spoke of it again. She knew at that exact moment that Jacob was the only man for her. He loved her flaws. Isn't that what everyone wants—to be loved not for your perfections but also your imperfections?

Beverly never saw herself as a mother but dreamed of having children with Jacob. She wanted to raise a child with the man she loved. She desired nothing more than to share their endless love with a little version of themselves. She was never able to carry a baby to full term. She had several miscarriages that ended in heartbreak, each one more painful than the last. The physical toll on her body became too much for her, and sadly, that dream never became a reality. Those were the cards that had been drawn, and adoption was not something Jacob would consider. I was in tears at this point in the story. She would have made a lovely mother.

After they moved to New York City, she continued to be involved in charity work, and Jacob continued to grow in his career. He was now at a point with his firm where travel was expected in his higher position. She joined him on his journey, and they traveled to cities around the globe. Jacob had a work ethic very similar to her father's, but he made time to explore every city with her. It was very rewarding for them both. She became more involved in different causes around the world. She was making a difference. She never thought a girl from New Orleans would dream of doing the things she did.

I could write a book on just her travels. She didn't want to miss out on anything in life. She made friends around the world, most of whom have passed away and traveled to God in peace. The look in her eyes was bright, but as she told the story, I could see the flame flicker. The blue started to fade, her eyes swelled, and her lip quivered. Beverly had told this story before, and it was not an easy task. Time was catching up to her. She was in a battle with time, and time would always win. Every breath was a battle she was slowly losing. Time tore her down with every swing of the sword. Then I figured it out. Beverly was sick. She was telling me her story for her life to continue. Beverly wanted to tell her story to people she felt would remember it, cherish it, and pass it along. It was important to her, and I was lucky enough to be one of those people.

Beverly and Jacob settled down for retirement in a house outside of New York City. They created a wish list of all the places they had not visited together. They lived out the rest of their days visiting two locations every year. He passed away two months before their trip to New Orleans. He died peacefully in his sleep. Beverly lovingly held him tight against her chest and carried his soul to Valhalla. Her hero was dead. Jacob had lived a full life, and she accepted that. She was sad, she was here alone, she was brave, and she was the last warrior left on the battlefield of life.

Beverly had no friends in New Orleans, no family, and no children of her own. What she did have was the fortitude to travel here alone. She checked New Orleans off their list. If I did the math right, she had been married to Jacob for over fifty years. I never asked her exact age. A lady never reveals her age, and a gentleman never asks. Every time she said his name, you could feel that she loved him very much. She had found her one true soul mate. If everyone could be that lucky, this would be a different and better world. A love that is timeless would be an easy clock to watch.

I sit behind a desk and listen to people all day. I answer questions, and I offer my services. I'm present, and I'm here for the guest. Beverly was here for me. What started out as a crazy warrior lady giving me a stern talking to, turned out to be the best story I've ever had the privilege of hearing. I had expected a conversation with Grandma and got a foul-mouthed old lady on a mission.

Just in case you're curious, she did everything on her wish list while she was in New Orleans. She was so proud of herself. She went on tours, explored museums and art galleries, and ate—oh, did she eat. She even took the ferry to where her parents' old home had been. The house is long gone, and where it once stood is an empty overgrown lot, full of memories. Beverly could still see her father sitting at the dining room table, eating alone. Her mother was ironing clothes on an old board in the corner of the kitchen, while holding her side in pain. She was smiling from ear to ear and singing her favorite song.

Beverly never once asked for anything difficult or for any special treatment. She ate at the dirtiest dive bars in the city and proudly danced at nearly every gay bar in the French Quarter. She stayed out drinking until 3 a.m. one night and got a ride back to the hotel from an older gay couple. They bought her drinks all night and a greasy cheeseburger on Bourbon Street. Beverly still had what it took to get men to buy her drinks, and she knew it. The day she checked out, we had one last conversation.

*

Beverly: I'm out of here. It was a pleasure getting to know you, young man. You keep up the writing and don't stop. I expect to see those plays on a stage near me soon.

Me: It was my pleasure getting to know *you*. I've never looked forward to talking to a guest every day. You're the first.

Beverly: Just promise me one thing, sport. Don't be scared to write a book one day, and don't let your fears get the best of you.

Me: I promise. Can I hug you?

Beverly: I'm a dirty old lady. You can do more than that.

Me: I'd be happy with a long hug.

Beverly: Bring it in.

Me: I don't want to see you go, Bev.

Beverly: I'll always be in your heart, my darling.

*

Beverly embraced me as if I were her son. She gracefully walked out the front door like she was walking on air. She creates a feeling of love around her. It's her gift to the world, and it's priceless. Her family is the world and the people she meets, her children. I gave her my information to stay in touch. She called me every two months to check on how my writing was progressing. For two years, she was a constant source of motivation. Even from a distance, I could feel her love radiating. Then one day the phone didn't ring. Two months and then six months passed, but I never heard from her again. She had left my life as quickly as she had entered it. Time had caught up. Her sword was at rest, and her battle had come to an end. Time did not win because I remember her. Lady Beverly of Awesomeshire is an immortal warrior.

Her last gift to me before leaving was an envelope. She slipped it into my hand and made me promise not to open it until she was long gone. Inside was a note that said, "Never fear your future," and wrapped inside the note was $500. It was the biggest tip I've ever received, but it felt like nothing compared to the time she'd spent with me. She made me want to do more with my life. I want to explore, be a better man, make a difference, live my life, love, tell my stories, and never fear my future. I used the money to buy this computer. I'm telling her story. I'm telling the story of Lady Beverly of Awesomeshire.

Bev, please know I heard you. I raise my frosted mug of cheap beer to you. I'm listening to loud music at a bar with sticky floors and great food. Standing next to me is my Jacob. The man I love. The man who is my endgame. I will never forget you, Lady Beverly . . . Bev. Thank you for sharing your life with me. I'm truly honored and blessed.

DINNER FOR ITALIANS

I wish every story was a sweet story, but life is not always sweet. That's what makes life interesting. *Interesting* is a "nice" word to explain what happened with this guest. There are certain guests who go out of their way to test your merit. They love to push your buttons to test what they can or can't get away with. This is a dangerous trap for any hotel worker. If you give certain guests an inch, they will take ten miles, half the kitchen, and free upgrades. They will do or say whatever they can to get what they want.

I've never understood why people would go out of their way to take advantage of a business or another person. Guests will say vulgar, degrading comments to your face and then feel this should be allowed because they're paying guests. Sometimes but not always there will be repercussions. I don't believe in rewarding bad behavior, but, sadly, most hotels will. Guests are paying for the pleasure of staying with us and somehow feel that includes abusing the employees. The act of treating you like a human being is second on their list. They know you can't open your mouth in defense, and they're waiting for you to do so. This is wrong on so many levels.

Guests can complain, lie about their experience, and receive anything they want from the hotel for free. It's a game guests play with hotel employees. Historically, hotels will throw the bank at an upset guest just to avoid a difficult situation, whether the guest is right or wrong. There is a boundary in customer service, and guests cross it often, but employees can't. Are all employees angels? No, they're not. You hear stories of awful employees all the time, but I'm not covering those stories in this book. Honestly, there are some deplorable employees on my side of the desk. I know we can be shitheads.

A hostile work situation can happen at any business in any work field. It still doesn't justify abuse from either side of the desk. Especially abuse from a guest. I've been working in hotels for years, and I can tell you that times are changing. Hotels are now doing more to protect their employees from sexual harassment and dangerous situations that guests cause. As a guest, you shouldn't make rude, obnoxious comments to a hotel employee. I can't stop you from being an asshole, but don't expect me to smile and take one for the team. It only makes you look like a jackass and makes me feel bad. I can report your behavior to a manager, and the appropriate action will happen. The climate in today's work force is changing for the better, and it's about time it did.

I'm pretty good at holding my own. I held my own with a guest who sexually harassed me to the point I wanted to punch him in the face. I still maintained a professional attitude and courtesy, but it wasn't easy for me, coming from a bartending background. I'm writing this in defense of all the employees who could not defend themselves.

Management had been getting reports of an older Italian gay man hitting on anything with a dick. He'd already asked several housemen and valets if he could orally pleasure them. He was staying with us for five days and spending close to ten thousand dollars for an elaborate wedding taking place on the property. We had to tread carefully so as not to offend him in any way. He felt that all the male employees were amenities to his stay. We are not. We do not come with the contract you signed with the sales department. He was an older gay New Jersey Italian man. He was extremely overweight and breathed heavily even when he sat down. He had a guttural tone to his voice with a very strong Italian accent. This story doesn't work unless you think of that voice in your head. Think of the worst mobster movie you've seen with the worst New Jersey Italian accent. You got that voice in your head? I'm going to refer to him as Vito. He was a man who equally gave me a good chuckle and the taste of vomit in my mouth. Vito was the poster man for sexual harassment.

Vito staggers over and plops his heavy Italian ass down on my desk chair. The chair groans as if a thousand-pound weight was dropped on it from the top floor of my hotel. I'm surprised the chair doesn't give away from the sheer weight of this rhino slamming into it. He lets out a very audible groan of pleasure as he looks at me and licks his tongue across his yellowed teeth. He smells of cheap cigars and bad whiskey.

Me: Good afternoon, sir. How may I help you today?

Vito: God, you're delicious.

Ewwww. I upchuck my lunch and hold back from spraying him with the well-deserved vomit a man of his nature should be given. He would have enjoyed it.

Me: Thank you, sir. Do you have a question that I may assist you with?

Vito: The bellman and valets couldn't help me out, but maybe you can?

I already know where this is going. My years of working in gay bars prepared me for that look. It's the look of a praying mantis about to eat its mate. Vito's eyes are boring into my soul, and I can see his greasy wheels moving. He's mentally going through his arsenal of offensive comments and preparing to attack. He's looking me over to figure out exactly which angle is the best. Here's a hint. None of them. I've been warned about Vito. I know exactly what he's going to say. I can push buttons just as easily as a guest can, but it sounds nicer coming from my Southern lips.

Me: I'm sorry my associates couldn't help you with your needs. It'll be my pleasure to assist you. What can I do for you?

Vito: I want to eat your ass. Can you help me with that?

I honestly was not expecting such a vivid image. Bravo to you, Vito. I'm rarely caught off-guard in any way. I was expecting the usual lame pickup lines. I am impressed with his gusto and total commitment to his perversion. Does he think that this is something he can request of me? He said it to intimidate me. He said it to get a knee-jerk reaction that he could later use against me. It doesn't work on me, my little Italian spud. He has a shit-eating grin on his face, which is what I'd expect from a request like this. I am not offended; I am amused.

Me: I'm sorry, sir. Can you repeat that? I want to make sure that I heard your request correctly. I want to properly assist in every way possible to the best of my ability.

I say this with an eye squint and pinch my lips together. I am not flirting. I am not going to let this type of moron off so easy. I heard exactly what he said, but I make it clear it doesn't bother me in the slightest. Game on, Vito.

Vito: You heard me. I want to bend you over this desk and bury my face in your ass.

Vito grins wide when he says it, gives me a little pervy giggle, and very noticeably adjusts his nut sack. You dirty bastard! Would you like a side of taint with that? Do you need dipping sauce? Are we talking about your whole face buried in my ass or just the tongue? Can I see your ass-eating license? What is the duration of this proposed ass-eating event? Do I have to be clean and shaved, or is this a service you provide before the actual eating of ass commences? Am I allowed to make an angle request, or do I just lie across my concierge desk and enjoy? May I groan, or is this a silent ass eating? Are other people who walk by allowed to have a taste, or is this strictly a one-on-one situation? Do I get a mint afterward? Does this go on my Trip Advisor score? Do you provide services to other city concierges, or am I special? Do I get paid in advance, or does my performance directly affect the tip I'll receive? I only accept cash tips, not the tip of Vito's forked tongue or the green tip of his gross dick. These are all questions that run through my mind when he makes this request. This is sexual harassment. I'm creating a dialogue in my head as a self-defense mechanism against it. It's not right, and it's not fair to me. With a hint of a nice tone to my voice, I gracefully respond to his request.

Me: I'm going to tell you a quick story, sir. I was much younger and quite dumb during my time as a bartender on Bourbon Street. I was approached and offered many services quite like yours. I was too scared to respond, too scared of losing my job, and too scared to offend my customers. It was not right then, and it's not right now. I was too scared to say anything, but I'm not now. I left the bar scene shortly after that to work here in a more professional environment. A place where I could feel respected and not like a piece of Saturday late-night street meat. Your request for a "special service" is denied. No, thank you, sir. Do you understand? Now, what age-appropriate bar may I suggest for you, sir?

I find using a few overexaggerated "sirs" sprinkled in my tone to be fun. There's also a feeling of empowerment when you can spit the word **sir** at a rude guest. Be sure to stress the S like a snake sound. The lip curl is also vital in saying it properly. Vito is stunned. I wasn't rude, but the backhanded compliment must have stung him. There are ways to speak to people that are professional, yet still deliver a nice sting. He adjusts his elephantiasis-size nut sack again and sits up in the chair. He is playing with his man berries to divert my eyes. It's not working, dude. His unibrow is flared, and he leans forward. I'm an expert of the emotionless blank stare.

Vito: I don't need an age-appropriate bar. I need to get laid. Do you know who I am? Do you know the amount of money I'm spending here?

First, I don't care that you need to get laid. I honestly don't want to ever imagine you having sex. I'm guessing you flop around until you find a wet spot and then go limp. The only way a foul man like you could get laid is by paying for it by the hour. A sex worker should charge you an excess-baggage penalty for being overweight. It's called the "ton of fun" fee. I'm sure you'd dispute that charge on your bill, too. I know who you are. I was warned by management. If you as a guest say, "Do you know who I am?" that just proves how douchey you really are. I know who you're not. You're not a person I respect, and you'll not gain my respect by acting inappropriately. Money buys a lot, but it doesn't buy respect. I know exactly the amount of money you're spending. It's an obscene amount of money for your niece's wedding. I haven't seen you with her even once. You've not walked in the lobby with her, gone to dinner with her, or even said her name. I'm pretty sure she loves your money more than you. You're the rich gay uncle. This wedding is your way of feeling like you matter and not like the gross pervert you are. Don't pull this shit with me. I'm telling your niece. Shame on you, pervy Uncle Vito.

Me: I'm aware who you are and what you're looking to get out of your New Orleans experience. This ain't my first time at the rodeo. I'm here to help you in any professional way I can that is deemed legal. I can give you suggestions for bars with backrooms. You can go there if you choose. I'm sure you'll get the most out of your New Orleans visit at those fine establishments.

Vito: I like a man who's direct. You make me so farting horny. I want your dirty ass served on a table with a good red wine. Come visit my casino in New Jersey.

My ass is only dirty Sunday through Tuesday and on holidays. Has Vito given me a compliment? I think he has in his own sick way. I'm so happy knowing that I'm able to make this insignificant Italian man horny. My life is complete. It was a compliment laced with sexual assault. My Latino ass will never be on a table. My ass is not on the "All-You-Can-Eat" buffet at your crappy casino. Plus, everyone knows you drink white wine with ass. I'm joking; don't drink any wine with ass. It doesn't pair well. Vito just slipped the fact that he owns a casino in there for what? To be cute? Does he think I'm an opportunist? There is no amount of money that will make me overlook his many faults, whether he owns a casino or not. Does that work on guys? You own a casino? That's so nice. I'm still not impressed. What impresses me is people who treat me like I'm a person and not a piece of prosciutto.

Me: Thank you, sir. I pride myself on being honest and up front with my guests. Your request is absolutely off the table. You own a casino. That's nice . . . for you. I don't gamble. I don't believe in giving my hard-earned money away to a slot machine or draining my savings on a dream that will never happen.

Vito: You're worthless to me then. I'm going to hit the bars on Bourbon Street. I'll get into something down there. And by get into, I mean ass.

Me: That sounds like a lovely idea. Let's get you a cab, so you can be on your way.

No shit? You meant ass? Are you looking for ass while you're in New Orleans? I had no clue that you're looking for ass. Why don't you tell me one more time what you're looking for? Let me guess, it's ass? I offered to get you a cab because I want you to get the hell away from me. You're disgusting. You make me feel slimy. It's not okay to treat people this way. What gives a person that sense of entitlement? Does he really expect me to just say, "Yes, sir! Here's a clean spoon and my dirty ass. Enjoy!"

Vito: Make sure that the driver has a tight hot ass.

Me: I'll do my best.

I grab the first cab I can flag down. Does the driver have a hot ass? I can't tell from the angle. He is Middle Eastern and attractive as hell to me, so let's go with yes. I feel bad for the driver. I'm sorry, dude, but he's your problem now.

Vito: I'll see you when I get back.

No, you won't. I'm making myself invisible. If I smell you get off the elevator, I'm dashing down the hallway. If I see you tromping your way toward me, I'll suddenly have a case of explosive diarrhea and dismiss myself for an extended period. Worst-case scenario, I'll use paid time off to avoid you until you've checked out.

Me: There's something here for everyone, and remember: what happens in New Orleans stays in New Orleans. Have a nice day, and enjoy our lovely city.

Vito: God, you're delicious.

Can Vito see how physically nauseous he's making me? I don't think he cares either way. Vito only cares about one thing, my ass. My big Latino ass.

I feel dirty. I go home and take a very long shower just to feel clean again. This conversation still lingers in my memory like a week-old fart. Men are disgusting pigs, and I should know, I'm one of them. I have dealt with harassment several times in my life but never this extreme. I can't openly use my voice against it, or I'll lose my job. Every person has a right to not feel belittled at work, whether it's by a boss, a customer, or a hotel guest. You should demand this human decency in the workplace. The fear of retaliation from a guest stops most people in the hospitality industry from making their voices heard. Life is short, and there's no time to live in fear. I report the conversation to my manager. The sales director talks to Vito about his inappropriate behavior. Yay for a company that cares!

Vito doesn't talk to me again. He walks by me several times, stomping his feet to get my attention. He stares me down, licks his lips, and snarls. I'm expecting that one day soon, his gay casino mafia will abduct me, throw glitter in my hair, then force me to watch Vito do horrible things to small creatures. I ain't scared. Bring it, Vito. For now, I'm the great Latino ass that got away. Eat me.

THE GREAT TRANS CLUB
CREDIT CARD SCANDAL

Did you know that I'm a superhero? I not only save lives, but I save marriages. I was asked to lie to a man's wife. Don't be judgmental, there's more to this story than a lie. I'm not totally comfortable lying for a guest, but I will.

Supermodel Devin was a very nice and very attractive man. He had the genes that only a mad scientist could have brewed in a secret government lab. Devin was six feet three inches, with broad muscular shoulders, big thick arms, a hairy chest, a great ass, and a perfect toothpaste commercial white smile. You could see his six-pack abs through his skin-tight V-neck white T-shirt. Devin was obviously hung like a horse, too, or he stuffed his crotch. My first thought was, *Take off your checkered shirt! Show me the goods!* Devin was a sweet guy packaged in a very masculine male body. Yes, I'm objectifying the hell out of him. I would lick every inch of his body if given the chance. I never met his wife, but she did talk to me over the phone like a wailing banshee until we became best friends forever.

Devin runs up to me one morning with a look of panic. Devin has just killed a thousand kittens. His flustered appearance only makes him look hotter. I am drooling and in desperate need of paper towels just to soak up the saliva. This man could've told me to jump off the Crescent City Connection Bridge, and I'd have done it. Why do you have to be so hot and nice? Damn you, Supermodel Devin! The conversation we have is unexpected. Pull yourself together, Ren. Focus on Devin's words and not his plump, perfect lips.

Devin: I have a serious problem. I hope you can help me.

Yes. Literally, whatever you want. Do you need me to put a leash on your one-eyed monster? Do you need a hug? Please tell me you need a long hug. Can I feel your pecs and abs? Stand here and talk to me forever. I want to get lost in your clear blue eyes. Will you be my sex toy? Damn it, Ren! I mentally slap myself.

Me: Good morning. I'm sure we can figure out a solution to your problem. What seems to be the issue?

Devin: I was in a gay bar last night, and my credit card was stolen by a woman or a man.

Yes! There is a God. Devin is gay. I don't have a shot in hell with him, but I can dream big. I can now die happy knowing that a gay Atlas does exist.

Me: I understand. Do you need to file a police report? Do you need assistance in reporting the theft to your credit card company?

Devin: There's no need to get the police involved. I canceled the card last night, but the bank alerted my wife. She knows the name of the bar that the card was stolen from but not much else. I need you to tell her it's not a gay bar. I know my wife. She's going to call you. I was in there with a friend she doesn't approve of. The name of the bar was XYZ bar.

Damn it! Devin is straight, and he has a wife. No, I don't understand. When you say "friend," what type of "friend" are we talking about? Why would your wife call me? Does she know what Google is? Why were you hanging out at a trans bar? Are you gay, or do you just go to gay bars for fun? Why do you want to tease the local gay men with your stunning good looks? It doesn't matter either way. I'm just being nosy. I'm so confused. I have so many questions running around in my noggin. I'm going into mental overload. What should I ask him without offending him? Should I be cautious of this situation? Should I lie to his wife? What is my name? Screw it. I'm a motherfarting superhero. Cue the music, smoke, and flashing strobe lights.

Me: This sounds like a delicate manner. I want you to talk to me like I'm your best friend. Is that alright with you? I don't want to accidentally tell your wife something wrong by mistake. I can help you with this situation but only if you're totally honest with me. What were you doing? What would you like me to tell your wife? Is there anything I should not say? Trust me, I'm extremely fast. I can change my story on the drop of a dime.

The look of relief on Devin's face is so precious. Dude, you're so fine. I just lifted a weight off his perfectly chiseled back. I love my job. The eye candy is a great perk. I pride myself on being as honest as possible in any situation. If you don't hold back the truth from me, then I won't hold back the honest answers from you. I'm telling a story about lying, so how can I be an honest person? There's a way. Life can be a conundrum of funny incidents that culminate in one big lumping pile of honest fun.

Devin: I love my wife, but she can be difficult at times. Late last night I was in a gay bar with one of my best friends. He's gay. I'm not. I thought it was a sports bar at first. It had a sports bar name. It turned out to be a trans bar. We had a lot of drinks. I had a flirtatious conversation with this lady who I realized wasn't a lady. She was an amazing person with a smoking hot body, and if I swung that way and was single, I totally would have banged one out. I love all people. One of my best friends is currently transitioning, so please don't think that's the problem, I just don't like thieves. He . . . she kept rubbing all over me, felt my ass several times, and tried to lift my wallet. I realized that she was playing me, and the situation made me uncomfortable. My friend wanted to stay so he could hook up with a guy he met, and I wanted to leave. I remember going to the ATM for cash. I left my card in the machine, started to walk away for only a second, turned back around, and my card was gone. I think he . . . she must have stolen my card. I reported it to my credit card company, and they texted an alert notice to my wife. She called and yelled at me thirty seconds later. I told her I was at a sports bar, having a drink alone. I couldn't tell her I was there with him. The short version, she thinks he wants to sleep with me or he's using me. He isn't; we're just friends. I'm not gay. I need you to tell her that it's a straight sports bar. I hate asking you to lie; it's just better for everyone if she doesn't know the whole truth. Can you do this for me?

He was even hotter when he rambled. How was that possible? There are times when you shouldn't lie, and there are times you lie to protect someone you love. The truth hurts. There's a reason why that's a saying. He wasn't trying to be malicious. He wasn't having an adulterous affair. He was hanging out with a gay friend. His wife was not homophobic; she was just a very jealous person. She had a right to be; he was luxury real estate in the gay world. Jealousy looks ugly on anyone, but I understand it. I'm guilty of nearly throwing myself at him. I can't imagine the number of women and men she bats away daily. He doesn't even look like he needs to work out; he's just built that way. I feel envious and sad for her. I do lie for Devin. Sorry, lady, I'm team Devin all the way.

Me: I appreciate your honesty. If I can be candid, you're a ridiculously attractive man. I understand her concerns. It's sweet you don't want to hurt her feelings. Don't feel bad asking me to lie; consider it as a friend covering for another friend. I can tell you're a good person. If she calls, it'll be my pleasure to help you. It sounds like she's putting you in a difficult situation. I admire that you aren't backing away from a friendship that's important to you. Whether that friend is gay, bi, trans, questioning, or the thousand other labels society could slap on it. I'll take care of the matter. This is just a case of a stolen card. She'll be my best friend by the end of the call.

Devin: That's really cool of you. Thanks, man.

Me: It's my pleasure. Have a wonderful day.

My father always taught me to stand up when you shake a man's hand. Devin pushes past my outstretched hand and gives me a suffocating long hug. My knees go weak. He has pecs the size of two perfect mountains. I don't want him to let go. He smiles big at me, takes a step back, nods his head, then walks away. He knows what he's doing. The view from behind is better than winning the lottery. It is like two juicy apples dancing down the hallway. The phone call from his wife comes exactly thirty minutes later. Well, shit. I cannot screw this up. There are better tips in this world than a cash tip. His hugs are one of them. Here I go.

Wifey: Hi, are you the hotel concierge? I need your help. I'm desperate. I don't know who to talk to about this situation. My husband is in trouble, and I'm not there to help him.

Me: Good morning. Yes, I'm the hotel concierge. What seems to be the problem that I can assist you with today?

I know exactly who she is and what she is going to say. My pow wow with Devin has prepared me with all the intel I need to avoid a bad situation. I hate being blind-sided by anyone. It's a recipe for disaster from the start. She sounds like a hawk, and I can tell that her voice has power. She pronounces every word perfectly. Certain words are very pointed, as if she's hitting a musical note. My ears are delightfully being entertained, and she sings beautifully. Although she starts the conversation in a high-pitched squeal that only a dog can hear, she slowly calms down.

Wifey: My husband was robbed last night in the French Quarter. His credit card was stolen. I received an alert from our bank. I can't believe this is happening. He's there on a business trip, not to be hanging out in God knows what dive bar. Have you talked to a man today about a stolen credit card? I just want to know he's okay.

Me: I understand your concern. I spoke with a man this morning concerning a stolen credit card and suggested that he file a police report. Would your husband be a very tall man with blue eyes? He was very polite.

Wifey: Yes. I'm so angry at him. He told me he was at a sports bar, and I don't believe him. I looked it up online, but I can't find much on it. Where was he? What type of bar is it? Do people get robbed there often? Did he look all right to you? Was he with a man or a woman? Is this something I need to come there and take care of? I'm so mad at him.

Whoa! Slow down there. Overexcited much? Wifey is throwing questions at me faster than a speeding bullet. I can't get a single word into the conversation. Her mind is spinning off into Crazyville. It is time to put on the conductor's hat and get this crazy train back on the track to Saneladyland. I do admire her spunk. If my modelesque husband were alone in a Southern city of sin, I'd be freaking out, too.

Me: I'll tell you everything I know. First, your husband looked perfectly fine this morning. I asked him how his day was, and then we briefly talked about him losing a credit card. I've seen him in the lobby several times during his trip, and every time he's been alone. Trust me, I saw him every time he passed this desk. He's so tall, it's hard not to notice him walking by. The bar you mentioned is a sports bar. It's located only a few blocks into the Quarter, and it's a very safe bar. However, as with any major city, if you leave your credit card behind, chances are it will get stolen. He made a mistake, he reported it stolen, and I'm sure he feels awful about it. He didn't feel that a police report was needed, and I agree with him. That's all it was. He's been nothing but a gentleman while here. I've lost a credit card before. It's frustrating to replace and hard not to have it, but it happens.

Wifey: Thank you. Ren is a unique name. Is it female or male?

I want to point out I didn't technically lie. It's a sports bar, but more of a trans-gay kind of sports bar. Omission of a word isn't really a lie, right? It's not a safe area of town to be in, but she doesn't need to know that. I know exactly why wifey is asking about my name. I know what she's fishing for. She isn't sure whether I'm a man or a woman. I've played the pronoun game before, and I'm very good at it. She's protective of her man. She doesn't care whether I'm a man or a woman, but she does care if I'm looking at him. They probably have so many gay friends and girlfriends that she feels the need to keep an eye on all of them. My best game play here is to kill her with open honesty.

Me: That's very nice of you. It was my grandmother's name. I'm a unique kind of guy. I have a great boyfriend. I want you to feel at ease, so let me just say that besides turning heads with our staff, he's fine. It sounds like you guys are on the same page, and nothing else is needed at this time. However, if you have any other concerns or questions, I'm here to assist you.

Wifey: Thank you so much. That does put my mind at ease. You sound like such a cool guy. I appreciate your honest answers. I'm a little overprotective, but you can imagine why. Keep an eye on him for me, if you get my drift.

Me: I get your drift. You're welcome, and have a nice day.

That, ladies and gentlemen, is how you do it. I didn't spill the beans on Devin, the supermodel, being out with his gay friend, which is what the guest requested, and I also made his wife feel comfortable from across state lines. I do feel a little bad for not telling her the whole truth, but that's something I can live with. We had a much longer conversation than what I highlighted, and she turned out to be a very cool lady. Granted, the conversation revolved mostly around her mouth-watering husband, but I didn't mind. She never enlightened me on exactly why she didn't like Devin's friend, but I get it. I protect my friends from anyone harming them, and she's protecting her husband. It is totally valid. Juicy drama must follow her everywhere. I see Devin only once more before he leaves. He is wearing designer jeans with no underwear that outlines his every long inch. The tight, extreme V, white tank top is busting at the seams. Devin does like to show off his package and big chest. He is rushing out to catch a flight.

Devin: Thanks, bro. You saved my life. I gotta catch a flight but wanted to give you a little something to show my appreciation.

Me: That's not necessary. It was a pleasure to assist you. I'm happy everything worked out well. Have a safe flight home.

He reaches out to shake my hand and instead grabs me, pulls me in for another big hug, and whispers, "Thank you," in my ear. I melt and again fall into his perfectly chiseled chest, as he pushes his pecs against my face and his crotch against my side. I feel "you know what," throbbing. No, thank you! He smells like a sweaty mountain man. If I could bottle his smell of musk, I would be a billionaire. I then feel his hand practically grope my ass, as his hand pushes something down into my back pocket. Did Devin just feel me up? Am I in some alternate reality? I can get used to this.

Devin: My wife said to give you a good tip; the hug was a bonus. Thanks, man.

Me: Thank you. Thank you so much. Have . . . have a nice . . . whatever, enjoy me . . . I mean enjoy our lovely . . . lovely body . . . ugh . . . city.

Devin: It was my pleasure.

Devin felt me up, and he totally just flirted with me. I was obviously too distracted from his sexually charged hug to respond appropriately, and he loved it. He gives me a little smirk, laughs, flexes his muscles, and walks out the door. I'm convinced he flexed his ass on the way out just to give me that one final tease. He knew I was watching him leave. I wonder, Did his wife tell him to give me the tip, or was this his sly way of giving me a little extra somethin'-somethin'? Damn you, Devin, for your evil ways! I reach into my back pocket and pull out a crisp one-hundred-dollar bill. It is warm and wet and smells like man musk. Yes, I smell it for at least five minutes. I may have even pressed it against my cheek for a moment. I have no doubt it was wrapped around his no-no place. I frame it in my mind as a reminder of my time with him. I don't work here for the tips, but who doesn't love a nice wet bill? Well done, Devin, you win the title of "How to Make Your Concierge Blush." Devin is a freak. There's no halo over Devin's head. Devin has horns. If he's the mayor of hell, then I'm moving in.

LADY V

Let's talk about the almighty VJJ, the beef curtains, the sticky entrance to the world, and the main reason most men act like dumb dogs. Yes, I'm talking about the almighty vagina. Big and in your face vagina, the capital V, the beast that drips blood once a month and doesn't die. It turns the sweetest woman into a fierce creature of death with enormous strength.

Let me introduce you to Lady V. She was in our lobby talking with friends and having a jolly good time. She sat on the couch directly across the lobby, facing my concierge desk, and wore a see-through white skirt that was not age appropriate. She had beautiful jet-black hair that would make even the most confident woman jealous. The carpet did match the drapes. How do I know this? Lady V was not wearing panties! She felt the need to lean back, laugh, and spread her legs, flashing her lady bits directly at my horror-stricken eyes every two minutes. I had front row seats to the show of the century and couldn't escape. My face was doing that pinched look you get when you're disgusted but trying to smile. We've all made that face at some point in our lives. It was so painful that I'd have rather eaten a bowl of lemons.

The penny peek show was lost on me, but bless her heart for thinking it wasn't. I'm a curious person. I'll look at the merchandise, but it doesn't mean I'll buy it. Lady V's lady lips were a train wreck. You know you should look away, but every fiber of your mortal being won't allow you to slight your sight. The almighty V glared at me from across the lobby like an angry beast peeking out behind a furry black bush, waiting to attack. It snarled at me, hissed, and

173

retracted when it sensed I wasn't interested in taking it for a walk. There is no leash long enough in this world or the next that would have held back this beast. Let me present it in such a way that you, the reader, can get the full understanding of my predicament. If I were in a snowstorm, cold and desperate, and my only chance of survival was to crawl inside her roast beef bed for warmth, I would rather freeze to death.

I didn't have much direct conversation with Lady V. It was more of a screaming match across the lobby. I never answered her in more than one or two complete sentences. The few incoherent questions that Lady V bellowed at me came across more like an old New Orleans restaurant barker. Every time Lady V opened her mouth to bark, it was like a bullhorn. She had zero volume control. Her laugh was loud enough to shake bricks loose from this old hotel's walls. Worse, she'd randomly screech, "Wooooooo!" which irritating drunk older women love to shout. They think they're the life of the party, but really they're just irritating everyone around them. Lady V would yell a question at me with no intention of hearing the answer. She screamed to grab my attention, then she gloriously and proudly displayed her gaping black overgrown lady garden.

Here's a tip for every tourist to follow when you're drunk off your ass in any city. Your friends are not laughing with you, they're laughing at you. The only reason they keep you talking is to hear what ridiculous new gossip you'll spill out of your flapping mouth. I have friends who make fun of me all the time when I talk, so I get it. However, a public lobby is not the best place to act like you're reliving your long-forgotten sorority days when "Oh. My. God. You were such a slut."

I digress; let's get back on topic. We're not here to talk about our past. We're here to talk about that cavernous hole Lady V felt obliged to share with the world. I'm sitting across from her and unable to escape the direct onslaught of the award-winning *Snatchtacular Show*. For the love of baby Jesus, Lady V, keep your legs closed. Why buy the cow when the milk is free?

Lady V: Wooo! How you doing over there, baby? I'm in New Orleans, and I feel good. Check me out! I'm drunk. I got a beer.

Me: Hello.

Oh, sweet lord, what the hell is up with this drunk cougar in my lobby? Lady V looks like a plastic doll squeezed into a white sheepskin condom. Wait a minute, are my eyes playing a trick on me? Is that a dark patch? Are you not wearing panties? Lady V is old enough to know the rules of fashion. You do not go commando in a short, white, skin-tight, see-through skirt. Yep! That's your vagina staring right at me. Oh, great! She feels the need to lean back and give me a better view of her baby under carriage. That's just not right! I don't want your hanging meat parasailing toward me. Please, double bubble-wrap it, and put it in storage already. The Father, the Son, and the Holy Ghost.

Lady V. It's my birthday! Look out, boys! Woo! I'm drunk. I'm pretty. What do you think about that, stud?

Me: Happy birthday!

Yep, that's now the fifth time she's leaned back and spread her legs. Do you not realize that the entire lobby can see your naughty bits? You're literally airing your puss-puss out for the world to see. Why would you wear white with that dark bush shining through like a beacon of light at midnight? Does it have teeth? Do you swallow young college men like an overeager saleswoman? I swear I hear a faint yelp of help coming from within. The call is coming from inside the womb, Carol Ann. I'd reach in to pull out that missing scared frat bro, but I'm afraid I would lose my arm at the shoulder.

Lady V: Why are you way over there? Come party with us. You're no fun. Wooo! I need to pee.

Me: Thank you for the offer, but I need to stay here to answer questions for all our guests.

My body is like a ship, and your cunt is like an ocean whirlpool. I can feel the pull from here, and I don't want to visit Davy Jones's locker tonight. Please stop yelling at me. You're embarrassing yourself. Why are other guests in the lobby looking at me like we're friends? We're not friends. Lady V, you have three friends sitting next to you who need to pull the reins on your drinking fun time. Oh, damn it! Did you just scratch your kitty? I definitely heard a sickly meow or an audible queef. Do you expect me to jump up, run over, and tame your feral cat? I'm going to throw up in this tiny trashcan next to my desk. I'd feel violated if you weren't so drunk, but I just feel sorry for you.

Lady V: I'm so drunk. Let's go to the restroom. Let's go to the bar. Let's go to Bourbon Street! Let's go find some men. I need to pee. Oh, my God, did I say that out loud? I'm such a classy lady. Am I being loud? I'm so drunk. Am I annoying you? Do you think I'm drunk? Hey, you! Do you think I'm drunk? Woo! I need to pee.

Me: Would you like a bottle of water?

If I see a wet spot on that couch, I'm going to punch you in the twat so hard your tits are going to feel it. I hate your friends. They're giggling and not taking care of you like real friends should. Did you just cup yourself like a five-year-old doing the pee-pee dance? I beg you, Lady V, get the hell up, stagger down the hallway, and make tinkle. You shouldn't have any problems pulling down your panties, because you're not wearing any! And that's the tenth time you flashed me your snatch. I'm done with staring at your black-covered pink flower. I haven't seen this much trim since I watched a straight porn in college. I'm done. I've never wanted to get up and walk away as much as I do at this moment. The Snatchtacular Show needs to drop the curtains. I give it two big thumbs down, but thanks for the laughs. Lady V then jumps up, stretches her hands up high, and yawns while yelling at her friends, "I want to go!" Peek-a-boo, there it is again. I vomit in my mouth a little, and it is not tasty.

Lady V: It feels so good to stretch it out. I can't wait to get to a bar with dance music! I'm ready to shake my ass and show these New Orleans men what a real woman looks like. Hey, you! Hey, boy! Where should we go to dance our tits off?

Me: Bourbon Street is always a good start.

Lady V: Let's hit it, girls. Bye, boy. Woo!

Me: Have a nice day, and enjoy our lovely city.

I don't think she can stretch it out anymore. That vagina rubber band snapped three decades ago. I mentioned in another story how much I loathe being called "boy." It holds true for this story, too. I cut her stank eyes that could kill. Lady V purposely stretches high to make her skirt lift and give me one final peek at pussyland. Ugh! You just had to play that hairy card one more time before you walked out the door, didn't you? I preferred staring at that folded-over fur baby of black-haired wasteland when you were sitting down. I didn't think the situation down below could get any worse, but I was wrong. What I'm looking at now was ripped right out of a science-fiction movie. It's just hanging there like two pieces of burnt rubber. A strong wind could catch her sails and carry her to the Land of Forgotten Cha Cha. Lady V needs to invest less in alcohol and more in a personal Kegel trainer. I pour a gallon of liquid disinfectant over my entire body and scrub my eyeballs with a wire grill brush. Lady V walks out the door with a wet-sounding squish to her bad catwalk stroll. She forgets to go to the bathroom. I laugh out loud, and people do stare. For I shall send Lady V into New Orleans, and the streets will run yellow with the urine of thy enemies. Lady V is just that classy.

BAE THE BRIDE VS. GRAY THE GROOMSMAN

I often feel like furniture in the lobby. I don't live on the same plane of existence as the guests who walk by and ignore my greetings. I can say hello ten times to the same people, and they'll ignore me every time. That is, until they desperately need something, and then suddenly my service is a matter of life or death. I'm acknowledged as a living, breathing human being, instead of lobby cannon fodder. I'm standing right here, but the guests can't grasp where I've been during their whole vacation. Why have I not assisted them before this very moment? They're having a restaurant emergency! I should have a table for twenty standing by at one of the top restaurants in New Orleans just for them. Plus, it should be private dining with a jazz band, a view of the sea, and someone to stick a finger down their throats when they're full.

Guess what? I did try to assist you, but your snooty ass was too self-involved to even acknowledge me. I'm sitting right here with a huge smile and a lifetime of experience to share with you. You can talk to me. I'm here to help, but you need to approach me. A concierge can make or break your experience, and all you need to do is open your mouth, say hello, or ask a question. We'll have an answer.

This will happen time and time again. This happens with the doctors, the students, the businessmen, the honeymoon couples, the football fans, the mean cheerleader moms, the bachelorette parties, the millennials with their stupid man buns, the teachers, the cruise families, and people of every race, color, age, ethnicity, sex, religion, and sexual orientation, whether they are highly educated or more "salt of the earth" types. It's a sad realization that you don't matter to most people, until you do matter.

The groups that do this most often are the bridal parties. They are the worst. I'm not hating on my wedding peeps. It's not all of them. I've talked to some kick-ass newlyweds, and I didn't want the fun to stop. I've taken pictures with them, fallen in love with the wedding couple, and made new besties. Sadly, though, it's the wedding parties that ignore me the most. I understand that you have a lot running around in your head, but how hard is it to say hello? I'm okay with a head nod; just acknowledge that I'm here.

I love most brides, from the mean ones to the steampunk brides, from the stuck-up million-dollar ladies to the happy bride who sewed her own dress. If you're super cool to me, I'm going to be super cool to you. However, I do ask that if you're going to constantly ignore me every time you pass me, then please do me the courtesy of ignoring me when you get into a screaming match with a member of your wedding party. I'm not a referee, and I will not take your side just because you're the bride. Look here, chick, if you're being a bridal nightmare to someone, and that person tells you to go fart yourself, then you probably deserve it.

Bridal Bae and the best man tore it down. I wasn't sure if I was in a hotel lobby or an illegal dogfight ring. I was an innocent onlooker, enjoying the show and keeping score. There's nothing better than being an observer to a catty fight. Gray was two snaps fabulous, and his sharp wit rivaled my own. Bae was a monster on heels and had the vocabulary of a sixth-grader. I was asked two questions. Luckily, I was not given the chance to respond to either.

I had the pleasure of just smiling big, while looking back and forth at them. I was a cat watching a fly dance on the wall.

I could tell from the very beginning of the fight that Bae the Bride didn't stand a chance against Gray the Groomsman. It was awesome. Some of the best stories I've heard are ones where I said nothing at all. A great concierge will be an observant spectator when he or she needs to be, but also the best player on the court when required. My popcorn is buttered, cold soda in hand, and my blank face is on point.

The fight started around the corner from my desk. I heard the loud clicks of mile-high hooker heels and a strong Southern gay accent, and I prayed to God that it would not involve me.

Bae: Did you hear what I said? Listen to me, you damn shit gay!

Gray: Girl, how can I not hear you? The accent of bitch is all anybody can hear. I'm going outside for a cigarette. Follow me if you dare.

Bae: Stop! You ugly farting stupid budget faggot. You can't talk to me that way on my wedding day and then just walk away from me. I want to know what's going on. I deserve an explanation.

Gray: I can talk to you any way I want! I'm not marrying you. He's my best friend, and I don't have to explain myself to you. Who the hell do you think you are?

Bae: I'm the bride!

Gray: You're a spoiled brat. There's not a single redeeming quality about you that I like.

Oh, snap! First point goes to Gray. I like this guy already. He has a little gay lisp that's endearing to me. He snaps his fingers every time he finishes a sentence, just to punctuate the end. They finally come into view and stand in the middle of the lobby, which happens to be directly in front of my desk. I'm guilty of pre-judging his voice. I was expecting a twink in a white fairy suit to appear, and instead it's a very masculine, attractive man. He has a beard and very strong stature. Bae is your typical Southern, bottle-blonde hair, blue-eyed, big-boobed, dime-a-dozen bride that you see in every bridal magazine. She has mascara running down her face. Obviously, she was too cheap to buy the tear-free, no-run type of mascara. Dollar-store makeup is a big wedding no-no. Just saying, if you had loved your gay more, then you wouldn't look like a dollar-store circus clown. I'm not stereotyping gay men, but we do have that shit on lock. Brides, be nice to your gays, or you're going to walk down the aisle looking more like a baboon than a bride. Why is Bae wearing booty shorts, a tank top shirt, and high heels? Again, she needs a gay bestie to save her from public fashion faux pas. Bae prefers to insult her gay, instead of showering him with kindness. Bae is angry-crying. I like it. I'd usually not advocate treating a bride poorly on her wedding day, but the "faggot" comment already told me that she was a piece of shitty artwork. Negative ten points to Bae.

Bae: You'll do what I say and when I say it, or I swear you'll never see Justin again! Do you hear me? You ass-eating horny goat weed! I don't care if you're his best friend or not.

Gray: I'd like to see that happen.

Bae: You farting, piece of shit, cock-sucking, dirty asshole prickhead. This is my special day, and you're ruining it. You ruin everything!

Gray: Your use of vulgar slang only emphasizes your lack of education. Justin and I have been friends before we had hair in private places. There's nothing you can tell him that will change that fact. We'll always be in each other's lives.

Yes! Second point to Gray. Who taught Bae to cuss? She's very bad at it. It's like Bae has a bowlful of cuss words written on pieces of paper. She pulls them out one at a time to string together vulgar sentences of hate that make no sense. Gray speaks very eloquently. He has a pocketful of very pointed quips to throw at her. He never once raises his voice or screams at her. He has an intentional way of getting his point across in a certain manner that only pisses her off more. He's not bothered by her slurs, and his confidence in what he says is not only impressive, but hella sexy.

Bae: That's it! You're not coming to my wedding. I don't want to see your worthless, smelly, butthole-licking, gay ass anywhere near us. I hate you! Faggot!

Gray: I'm the best man. I'm not here for you. I'm here for Justin. You've always hated me, so you can hate me for two more hours.

Bae: If you love him so much, then why don't you suck his dick and get over yourself? Leave him alone, donkey dildo licker, bitch ass. What do you think about that?

What do you think about that, Gray? Why is Gray not answering? Why are they both looking at me? Oh, shit! She's asking **me** that question. What do I think about that? I say, do it, Gray. Suck it. If Justin is half as cute as you, then go for it, dude. She sounds homophobically horrible. Do I answer her? I'm not taking a side in this wedding party shit showdown. This is not my fight. I don't know everything that happened before this moment. I only have a snapshot of what Bae's relationship with Gray is. Bae lost me as an ally when she started throwing out mean, gay-bashing, homophobic comments. She vomited them out of her mouth with too much ease. Bae is so far in the hole now that I've stopped keeping score. It's been my experience that if you can't control your words when you're upset, then the color of your soul is blacker than midnight. Bae is not a nice person or a nice bride. I start to open my mouth, and then Gray saves me.

Gray: Don't ask the concierge what he thinks. You're always stirring up shit with people. Leave him out of this. You're a drama queen. I give Justin a year before he sees your true self and hates himself for this mistake. We both know why he's really marrying you. Please stop lying to people about "love being blind" and your "pussy is magic." It's not. It's more like a doorknob: everyone's had a turn.

Bae: I hate you. Your democratic, fairy-dusting, gay, stupid, retarded ass is just jealous.

Seriously? When did politics get into this? Is calling someone **democratic** a cuss word now? When did that happen? That's a big word for her, and I doubt she knows what it means or if she's even using it correctly. I desperately want to pull her aside and school her in cussing. I have a hard time believing she was not a mean girl in school who spewed out rectangular-shaped insults like a candy dispenser. Bae is a decade out of practice. Fart! Can you get out of practice? Shit, maybe I need to cuss more. She's not only using every cuss word wrong, but she's also very politically incorrect in using them. How can one person be so bad at something so artful? My ears are bleeding. The belief that a gay man can sprinkle everything with fairy dust is not true. If that were the case, then every hot man would be gay. I could wave my magic wand and say, "Poof! Be gay. Now sleep with me." Also, let me slap you one good time for the retarded comment. It's rude, it's a slur, and polite society doesn't use that term—but you're not polite society.

Gray: Is that the best you got? For your information, Ms. Thang, I've seen him naked . . . many times. I've known him for thirty years. We grew up together. We jerked off to gay porn, straight porn, and had a dirty all-night threesome. He shot his stuff on my face more than once . . . and he liked it! We've even slept with the same girl on the same night, or did he not tell you that? I'm not that gay, and Justin is a winding country dirt road. This marriage is a farce. Sorry. That's a big word for you. That means it's a joke, a ludicrous comedy shotgun wedding, and you're welcome.

Bae: You lying, slut-bag, queer, homosexual, dog bitch!

Gray: You'll always be sloppy seconds, honey. The next time you get on your knees, you'll know I got there first. Hello. (Snaps!)

Bae: (Turns around to glare at me and asks . . .) How can you just sit there?

Wait, are you talking to **me**? (Cue Robert DeNiro in **Taxi Driver**.) If I were still keeping score, Gray just landed the finishing move. This game got really heated really quick. I love it, but I don't want to play anymore. Is my mouth open? I'm literally holding my jaw from hitting the floor. I feel like I'm listening to a trashy fight on tape. How did he say all of that with a serious face and not laugh? I am waiting for him to twiddle his fingers together and laugh like an evil genius. I shake my head to clear away the fog and step back into reality. Again, are you talking to me, Bae? I'm just a piece of furniture. You've ignored me every time you passed me. The only time you even spoke around me was to say, "It's so hot in this city. I hate sweating. I hate this city. I hate all these ghetto-ass dirty people here." You didn't say that directly to me, and I thank you for that. But you did say it loud enough for everyone in the lobby to know how much of an uber privileged princess you are. And now you want me to be your friend? Protect you from this man who I think is super awesome? You want me to defend your honor when you don't have any? That's not going to happen, sweetie. First, you're both lucky there are no kids in this lobby, or I'd have called security. Second, who am I kidding? I wouldn't have called security. I'm loving the show. Gray deepens his voice, spins around, snaps twice, rolls his head, and clears his throat. You can always tell when a gay man is about to read the hell out of someone when he physically prepares himself for the onslaught of honesty that is about to be bestowed on his victim.

Gray: How can he just sit there? Because it's not his job to care about your feelings. You followed me all the way from your room just to cuss me out. This again just shows how tactless and classless you are to be having this fight in public. I was talking to Justin, not you. All I said was that I was going to be in Justin's life forever. He's my best friend, and I'd take a bullet for him. I've been there for every important moment in his life, and I always will be. I told him my honest opinion about this marriage, and I don't care if you like that or not. Yes, I told him I loved him because I do love him. Why is that so wrong for you to hear? I was there before you, and I'll be there after you. I understand that things will change after you're married. But you had no right to dictate to him, in front of me, who will or will not be allowed to be in his life. Do you understand how shitty that is to put him in that position? You forget it's his special day, too. You started this fight, and now I'm going to end it. I'm going to walk outside, smoke, and forget we had this conversation. You can go back up to the room and finish your clown makeup. Fair warning: if you follow me outside, things will get ugly between us. I don't think I'll be able to control what I'd say.

What? Things are not already ugly? How much uglier can they get? This is a symphony for my ears! My eyes are the size of Mardi Gras doubloons, and my blank stare is on point. I raise my eyebrows and bite my lip. You're cold as ice, dude. I need to admit, he turned me on. I've so much mad respect for Gray right now. Justin is his best friend. Gray is defending his friendship. Granted, Gray is doing that in a super bitchy way to the bride, but I love it. I love when people don't hold back on what they really want to say to each other. I doubt Gray and Justin's relationship is as sex filled as he made it out to be, but it was hot as hell to hear. Bae is weeping like a newborn baby who has been smacked on the bottom for the first time. She has gone from angry-crying to ugly-crying. It's that type of crying where tears are gushing, her lips are curled, and she's breathing heavy with those little baby hiccups mixed in. Don't ugly-cry, readers, it's gross. She's crying so loud now, it's sad to witness. If you hadn't heard the entire conversation, you might feel sorry for her. Then I realize, not one single person has come down to check on where the bride is. Does everybody in the wedding party despise her? How in the hell did this marriage ever happen? I don't buy her performance, and I don't give two shits about passing her a tissue. Ding. Dong. The witch is dead.

Bae: I can't deal with you right now. It's your kind that's ruining this world. You're a hateful, ugly, pig-boy whore slut.

Gray: Bye, Felicia!

It's "your kind" that's ruining this world? If she meant "your kind" as in a loving person who stands by his friends through the bad times and good times, then I say, "Ruin away." Can I point out how awesome it was that he ended the conversation in the gayest way possible? It was music to my soul to hear a masculine man with a lisp utter those words. I giggle out loud. Bae cuts me a look that would have separated my head from my shoulders if she could. She storms off with a click-clack that is deafening.

Bae: Bye, bitch!

I'm unsure whether that was directed at him or me, but I never see or hear from her again, and I was listening for those mile-high hooker heels. Gray looks at me and smiles beautifully. He has a perfect white smile. The God of Dentistry is his best friend. He walks over to me, and we begin a long conversation about what just happened. He apologizes for the ugly disturbance. I say that I understand, but in the future, please refrain from having such a graphic conversation in the public spaces of the hotel. Gray laughs and agrees that it won't happen again.

He comes back to talk and flirt with me over the next couple of days. We share some good laughs and swap stories. I love a good secret, and Gray lets me in on the big wedding dirt. Bae is pregnant. Justin is marrying her out of obligation. Gray told Justin not to marry her, and that's where the big feud between Gray and Bae began. I knew there had to be more to the story! You don't unfold an argument like that in public unless there is a damn good cause. Gray admits that Justin and he jerked off once together when they were high. That doesn't count, does it? What's a bro friend for if you can't jerk off with him? They barely remember doing anything together. It was awkward for the next few months between them, but it never happened again. Gray had just discovered his bisexuality and hadn't been with a man yet. Who better than your best friend to have your first gay experience with? The rest of the graphic details were pure fiction. I can relate; a good story needs a little fluff.

Before Gray leaves, he introduces me to Justin. He is a cute, rugged, slightly beefy man with a tired appearance. He appears to be moderately wealthy by the way he carries himself. I can understand from his nature why he is marrying Bae. I don't agree that two people should get married only because of a pregnancy, but I get it. It's an honorable thing to do, although not always the right thing to do. Gray and I became close friends that weekend. We stay in touch through social media, and I cherish of all our conversations.

*

It was about a year later when I got a long message from Gray. Justin and Bae were divorcing. She wanted nothing to do with Justin or the baby boy, whom they named Stone. It was Gray's favorite baby name. It was not the reason for the divorce, but it must have pissed Bae off. I feel bad for little Stone. He'll grow up without a mother figure in his life. When there's no love in your mother's heart, is it better for her to stay or go?

Bae gave up all rights to him, left, and said she wouldn't be back. Justin was going to be a single dad—or was he? The last time I talked to Gray, he was moving in with Justin to help raise Stone. I guess all things happen for a reason. Gray and Justin are going to be together now, in a strictly platonic way. How cool is that? Most people are lucky to have one loving, caring father, and this kid will have two.

Love is hard to define. The dictionary doesn't do it justice. You can't Google the answer, and it has a very different meaning to each person. I like to think of love as a light—it radiates from within. It fills your body with warmth and envelops those around you. My heart fills with this light whenever I think of this story. It may have started with hate, but it ends with love conquering all. Stone is going to have a very loving upbringing. I tell this story to showcase not what happened but the love that resulted from it. Love your family and your friends with your whole heart, and that love will be returned tenfold. Love is the force that drives you forward, makes you whole, warms you, and brings light into other lives. Love is . . .

A PIGEON AND HIS LADY

There are a couple of extremely hot months in New Orleans where you can cook an egg on the sidewalk. The intense heat is so bad that by the time you walk one block, you're covered in sweat. Humidity is enemy number one. I need to take two showers a day, or I smell like last week's tuna salad. It's not pretty, ladies and gentlemen.

It's also the slowest time of the year for tourism. My job is boring during these months. I often sit in the void of my hotel's lobby and count how many holes are in the ceiling tile above my head. There are 1,468 and two scratch marks. You wanted to know. I catch myself holding the guests hostage for conversation. I need the company, or my crazy thoughts will turn me clinically insane. I'm very creative at keeping myself occupied, but I've learned in life to never tell my boss I'm bored. If I do, I'll be cleaning baseboards, performing odd jobs, or worse: have my work hours cut. My hourly pay may suck, but I still need it.

I don't have large crowds of random people to talk to or conversations of great substance to overhear. My mind starts to wander. I look for any adventure around me. I've raced a penny and a quarter across the floor just to see which one would hit the wall first. The quarter usually wins, but the penny is a close second. When I say any adventure, I mean that literally. It can be from a strong wind blowing a dead leaf across the lot to a brave cricket hopping across the motor lobby. I ran outside many times to save Calvin the Cricket from getting squashed by the next random car pulling up. It's a game for me. I'm getting good at it.

It was during one of these slow periods that I noticed two interesting individuals—the first being a wretched-looking pigeon. This pigeon looked like someone had mauled him, dipped him in cow shit, pounded him into the ground, crushed his tiny legs, then picked him up, and repeated the process. It was the ugliest damn bird I've ever seen in my life, and that's coming from a kid who grew up in the country next to eight chicken houses. His eyes were milky white, and he routinely walked into the potted plants. He clucked like a chicken every time he hit them, and it made me giggle. He was so ugly that he was cute. The other birds would not come near him. They avoided him like the plague, or maybe he was just too ugly to acknowledge. He strutted around like he owned this luxury hotel. He was the big chief of the flying rat patrol in New Orleans, and he knew it. Let's call him Butch for this story. Butch could kick your ass. Butch had been in bird prison, and he survived his hoe check.

The second interesting individual I noticed was a little sadder. She was a homeless woman I saw routinely stalking around the property. For the purposes of this story, let's call her Mae. I never asked her name, and she never volunteered it, but she looked like a Mae to me. Mae was an older black woman with graying hair. She was simultaneously very aware of her surroundings, while not paying attention to anything important. Her eyes were always darting from one point to another like she was a spy surveying her surroundings for snipers. She looked heavyset, but over time I realized it was the six layers of clothes she always wore. She wore them well. I do have to give her two snaps for her tennis shoes. They were an old pair, but they were always immaculate. I was 99 percent sure she spit-shined them daily. She had pride in her one prized possession, and that gave me joy. I smiled because I loved seeing her. I frowned at the thought of having a comfortable life, while she did not.

Mae is one of the many reasons that I'm grateful for everything I've worked hard to achieve. I've earned everything in my life, but I still feel that I don't give back enough to others less fortunate than myself. Charity is important to your soul and keeps the mortal coil of the universe from spinning out of control. It may not be the essential element in the great secret of life, but it's extremely important to life. When we lose charity for others, do we also lose our morality?

Our struggles in life make charity toward others harder and harder to achieve every year. It's not math, and there is no right answer, but the willingness to be charitable to one another is achievable. I'm tired at the end of my day. It's easy to go home and forget everything else happening in the world. I do my best, but I don't do enough. It's not right, but at least I'm honest in this. I find that the older this world becomes, the less human beings care about one another. I fear that charity will go out of fashion one day, and the next generation will forget what charity was. People are so quick to cuss, scream, and yell at one another, instead of slowing down and seeing the situation in a different light or through someone else's eyes. Mae taught me to see.

I'm lucky to have a door and a window near my desk. I'm at arm's reach from the world outside. I'm lucky because on the days we have chili in the employee break room, my poots do be powerfully stinky. I'm not so lucky when there's a dust storm. I get a toxic facial of dirt, pollen, and Lord knows what else blowing in from the already smelly New Orleans air. It's a trade-off, and I accept that.

I look outside, and I notice this odd couple. Why have I never noticed them together before? Was I not really seeing the world around me, or was I choosing to be blind to what was in front of my face this whole time? How long has this been going on? Mae and Butch have a very special relationship. It is more like they are married to each other. Mae is sitting outside on the patio set. We have a tiny little outdoor area that is accessible to everyone, not just our hotel guests. That is her spot, and she claims it daily. The only other living creature she shares it with is Butch. Mae and Butch will be out there for hours together. She'll sit and talk to him like an old long-lost friend. She always shares what little food she has, and Butch is grateful for his scraps.

I often wonder what those long conversations are about. Is she telling him her life story? Can he understand her? Who am I to say he can't? He looks at Mae, clucks, pecks, tilts his head, and whistles. He is training her. His every movement is a clever way of gaining her trust and attention. What a clever little bird. That is his human, and he loves her. He talks back to her at times, or at least that's how it looks. They have mastered the art of bird-to-human conversation, and I am extremely jealous.

Butch is also very protective of her. I've never seen a trained attack bird. When someone walks by, he sits on the table and gives the passer-by the milky evil eye. Butch doesn't like other people. I am waiting for the day he attacks a guest and pulls out a bloody eyeball. The guest will scream, "Murder!" then fall to the ground in a bloody heap. I imagine Mae and Butch will both menacingly laugh, and then Mae will kick the guest in the face, do the sign of the cross, and quote Shakespeare, all while Butch dive-bombs the guest with poop. Maybe I'm the violent person? Nah! I'm totally normal for having these thoughts. Screw that guest for interrupting their precious time together.

This goes on for weeks, and I finally need to know. Curiosity killed my cat. He has been dead a thousand times over at this point, so what is one more time? What the heck is this unlikely duo doing and why?

One day I casually stroll into the kitchen and explain that I'd like to offer the lady outside something to eat, and they give me a couple of day-old hot croissants. I figure this is the best way I can get in good with Mae and Butch. The way to my heart is through my stomach, so why should it be any different for them?

Mae is sitting there talking so sweetly to Butch. I present the bread to her like it is a gourmet meal served on a silver platter. They ignore me. I place the croissants gently on the table and carefully bump them forward. She looks at me, smiles, nods her head, and turns back to Butch with a croissant in each hand. He looks at me very approvingly, chirps once, and doesn't fly away. She continues with her conversation as if I'm not even standing there, while she throws croissant pieces to Butch.

Mae regales him with stories of her life in New Orleans, the good times and the bad. She often edits herself and changes the narrative quickly, which makes it a little hard for me to comprehend. I am very intrigued to hear the stories she weaves with this little vagrant bird. She has had a rich life, full of adventures. What has brought her to being homeless? She won't answer any of my questions, but it gets me thinking about her mental stability. She is obviously a smart woman by the way she speaks, using a vast vocabulary. How did she get to this moment in her life? A homeless educated woman in a nation that prides itself on being the land of milk and honey. How is mental illness not a topic we talk more about?

Over the next several weeks, she stops by, and I bring out food for them both. Mae and Butch have a spiritual connection, and I am only a simple instrument in their orchestra. I often see Butch sitting on the table, looking right to left, patiently waiting for Mae to appear. She always arrives around the same time of day with a bright smile on her face. The sun casts its glow on her as she greets her friend. She is only interested in two things: feeding Butch and telling him stories.

Then one day I notice Butch but no Mae. It is the same the next day and the next day and the next day. Butch starts to look a little thinner, sadder, and I can tell that something is wrong. His friend is missing. I try to feed him, but he refuses to eat anything I have to offer. Is he starving himself, waiting on his friend to feed him? He flies around the property, searching for Mae with his milky eyes, but never finds her. Butch lies on the table all day but to no avail. I try to talk to him, but I am not his human. I am not his Mae.

Butch disappears a few days later, and I never see him again. I don't know what happened to either of them. I cry every time I think of this story. I wish I could find them both and shelter them in a better world. I wish I could place them in Eden with all the food they can eat and all the time in the world to just chirp and tell their stories. In a perfect world, there would be no homelessness, no sadness or pain. The world would be full of free bread and wonderful stories. This little bird made Mae's world a little brighter and his life not so solitary. I'm grateful for that one summer that I got to know this pigeon and his lady. For me, I went back to racing quarters across the lobby floor and saving crickets from cars. Poor Calvin didn't always get saved, but I tried. It may not be much, but it's charity for the greater good.

SPICES AND DILDOS

Yep. You read that correctly. The title of this story is "Spices and Dildos." I love to laugh with guests, and there was no shortage of giggles with this lady. Her name was Toni. She was a sexual airhead, and she owned it. She was very clever about it, proud of it, and flaunted it. Own the power you wield, and make it your weapon. Screw anybody who doesn't see that special gift, even if it's a gift that most people would ridicule. I have a friend who never thinks before she speaks. It makes for great blackmail material later. Do you think I don't write that shit down? Think again, my friends.

Toni thought before she spoke, and every word was on purpose without it sounding contrived. I could already tell I was in for one hell of a vocabulary ride on the dictionary freeway to hell. My dad always said, "Son, if you can't make fun of yourself, then you can't make fun of others." This is true. We're all dumbasses at times. We all do stupid shit, make mistakes, and say things that we should get kicked in the crotch for. If you can joke with yourself, then you'll always have a captive audience.

Toni was a middle-aged woman, dark hair, dark eyes, and just about as plain as plain can be. She spoke with a loud, confident voice for the world to hear. A powerful voice should always be heard. But remember, you're asking a total stranger for spices and dildos. When asking a concierge for sensitive products, do it with a hushed voice. Also, when you ask your concierge for spices and dildos, please make sure to ask for them in two separate sentences. I get it. Commas are hella hard. I over-use the shit out of them, but you're opening yourself up to an eyebrow raise and a lot of questions about your sexual practices. It raises a freak flag. Lucky for you, I love freaks. Oh, Toni, bless your smart little airhead heart.

Toni: Hi. I have something very special and delicate I need your help with. I need to wrap my hands tight around a few items. You look just like the person who can help make this happen for little ole me. I need different sizes, flavors, and textures. I need them to be affordable and comfortable for everyone. I want them hot but just right. I won't be using them. They're gifts, and I have no idea where to get them.

I feel dirty. What the hell are you describing? Are you asking me to run around town looking for specialty toys? Textured for her pleasure or his? What can be flavored, in different sizes, comfortable, a gift for multiple people, and large enough to wrap your hands around? You want what hot? It sounds scary. The images running through my brain right now are unimaginably delicious. Read what I wrote with a gutter mind, and you'll see why I am smiling. Toni is shooting herself in the foot with every dirty little word that escapes her naughty little puckered lips. I can't let this one slip away. I'm the king of subtext, and my dirty mind is having so much fun right now. Who says "little ole me" anymore? Do you want to sound dirty? I'm on board, if it comes with a paddle to the buttocks. Did my horns just pop out of my skull? I think they did. Cue the evil laugh.

Me: I'll be delighted to satisfy your every request. I'd be happy to put my hands on whatever you desire. There is no job too big that I can't handle. I'm positive that I can find the perfect size and flavor for all your friends' needs. The texture is up to personal preference, but I always like it a little rough. If it doesn't burn my hands, I like it hot, too. What exactly is it that you're requesting me to find, and how may I help you slip it in your hands?

I say it very fast, and I may have laid it on a little thick. I can tell her wheels are slowly turning. She is trying to comprehend what the hell I just said to her. Or maybe she knows exactly what I said and is searching her dirty mind for the exact thing to say back. Dirty minds do think alike. I am not trying to be a smartass, but if you're going to give me that much of a lead in, then I'm going to take advantage of it. There's nothing better than saying something so wrong in just the right way.

Toni: Spices and dildos. Isn't that cute!

Me: What?

Toni: I need to create special gift baskets for my "friends." I know they can use them because they aren't getting it anywhere else. I may even have a little left over to mix the lube and spices together, or I'll keep it all for myself. Hmmmmmm. I think that would be a perfect combo and so original of me. I could use gift tissue paper and baskets. I need different dildo sizes because a few of the ladies are heavy. Oh, who am I kidding? Let's just say it, they're obese. I don't mean to be sassy, but I may need to get a heavy-duty toy for Shelia. I don't even like that bitch, but she needs the tool and a strong beer. The spices should be local, and I want them to have heat. Can you direct me to a shop for these items? Do you know what I mean? It needs to be classy but naughty in one tight package, just like me.

Do I know what you mean? I'm hella confused. Where do I start? First, why are you talking to yourself and talking to me in such an abstract manner? I thought we were having a conversation, but it looks like you're having a whole other conversation with yourself. Did you just slam your friends by saying they aren't getting any? I guess a plastic toy boyfriend is better than nothing at all. Poor Shelia. She's gonna be getting the budget-store dildo that shorts out when she sweats. Please give that gift to her somewhere other than my hotel. This is an old building, and I don't want a five-alarm fire starting from a flaming plastic penis. FYI, you're making me smile from ear to ear, lady. Second, you're trying to figure out private gifts for your friends, yet you're saying it out loud to me in a public space. I was not expecting that very detailed yet vague response. I want to make sure I heard you correctly, so please repeat. I always ask guests to repeat themselves, not only to confirm what I heard, but to hear it said out loud again. I'm cute like that. Your friends are so obese, they need jumbo-size silicone fellas? Why the hell would you think that's the perfect gift? It's obviously not the perfect gift. Toni, you do know that spices and dildos are the most random gifts ever. They don't marry well, but to each their own. Third, you want to mix the lube with the spices? Do you mean to literally mix the spices in the lube? Do you know how bad of an idea that is? I've heard of a woman having a hot snatch, but this is next-level shit. You're raising the bar on gift giving. Is this the reason why it's called a "fire crotch"? I need more girlfriends who can keep me in the loop. I don't know who to feel worse for: the lady or the dildo.

You literally want them to burn? I can see it on your face, Toni. You aren't fooling me with your sweet smile and evil questions. Why don't you splash hot sauce directly in their cooch? It would be kinder. It'll also save you money and time, and you won't need to soak dildos in a vat of liquid heat. Do you hate all your friends or just Shelia? Finally, bless your heart, Toni. You're going directly to hell. No worries, though, I'll be sitting next to you. We can share a giant bag of frosted mini dicks while the sweet tunes of "Zero Farts Given" is playing in the background. You're such a smart, mean, airheaded, sexually charged woman that I don't know how to handle you. It's obviously not with gloves because you like it bare-handed and open-palmed. Where's my paddle when I need it?

Me: I can send you to separate stores to pick up those items. However, I don't know of one shop that sells both. There are adult shops in New Orleans to provide you with everything you need for all sizes of women. Also, I can recommend excellent spice shops, but I've never seen adult toys in a spice shop. I hesitate to give you other ideas unless I can speak frankly to you. I don't want to make you feel uncomfortable.

Toni: Of course, I just asked you for spices and dildos. I think we're well past the uncomfortable phase. I'm being so naughty. I need it, and I need it bad, stud. Please give it to me, and don't hold back. I mean the gifts. Yes. That's what I mean . . . the gifts. I'm such a stinker.

She smiles, giggles, and winks at me. I'm used to ladies flirting with me. Once you're asked why your balls are so big, then everything else seems tame. There's not much that fazes me. I look at her with conviction in my thoughts and a determination not to be outdone. Flirting is an art form, and I'm an old master. Toni is messing with me. People don't speak this way by accident. She knows exactly how suggestive she sounds. Don't get me wrong. I'm loving the visual images she's painting. Keep on dirty talking to me, and you'll see a magic trick. "Attention, ladies and gentlemen! Watch as the amazing Ren lifts the concierge desk eight inches in the air and never touches the desk with his hands." Toni, you're a raunchy, sexual, airheaded lady. I bet you give amazing spankings. "One, two, three, who's my bad little boy?" If I say the wrong thing, are you going to call me a bad name, then flog me with your wicked cat-o-nine tails? My safe word is **pineapple**. This whole airhead thing you're rocking is just a character you play for the men, isn't it? I got your number, Toni. You're not an airhead, you're calculated. I love a good game of cat and mouse. Play on, player.

Me: You're not a stinker. I think your ideas are cute. May I offer my professional opinion? I would tweak your idea a little, so as not to offend any of your friends. We can put together a great treat basket for all your friends without adjusting for any "larger" ladies. I do think that sensitive items like this should be bought by you and not me. I have no problem walking into a store and getting these items, but in my defense, I couldn't tell you the difference between a jackhammer and a lady tickler. We're all unique, and what satisfies one may not satisfy another. Instead, get the same toy for everyone. Maybe you can get an item that teases more than pleases. That way you get a laugh and not a grimace. Does that make sense?

Toni: Yes. That totally makes sense. You're so fun. You mean like a one size fits all? I didn't think of that. What girl doesn't like a tease? And the spices? Where can I get great local spices and lube?

Why does my job constantly involve vaginas? Is it because I'm gay, and women just automatically think that doesn't gross me out? If anything, it should gross me out more. I don't want to think about a one-size-fits-all vagina toy. I gave my best girlfriend an adult toy once. I never asked about it again, and I never will. I didn't even know there was a one-size-fits-all toy. I don't want that image burned into my skull, but thanks to Toni, now it is. Out, demons! Out! Toni is listening to me like I'm a sexual guru. I'm just spit-balling here, but she's giggling and doing the kiddie dance of joy. Every child does this dance when you buy him or her a shiny new toy. They don't pay me enough to deal with this. I'm slowly melting into a puddle of goo just talking about it. "Cleanup on aisle four!" I have no idea what spices would pair well with dildos. It's not like pairing a fine wine with a foreign cheese. I can reach out to ask other concierges, but I'm sure the answer would be the same as mine. Local spices are the easy request; you can get them on every corner. You want local lube? Not going to happen. We grow a lot of stuff here, but there aren't lube farms in New Orleans. Go into any grocery store and pick up a bottle like the rest of us. These topics were not covered in the concierge services orientation class. If they were, then I missed the day they handed out the secret sex handbook. It looks like I'll be faking one more thing in my life.

Me: I would forget the baskets and get empty beer sixpack holders. You'll have six little empty areas to fill with whatever you want. There can be a toy in one, lube in the other, one local craft beer for Shelia, a mini bottle of champagne, and two slots left for spices. I would play it safe and get a bottle of Tabasco and Tony's All Spice. Tabasco is made near New Orleans, and everyone loves Tony's. You can't go wrong with either of them. Another option would be locally made shea butter. There are several vendors in the French Marketplace that sell different sizes and scents. Trust me. Your friends will love it. That stuff is a miracle in a jar! Plus, let's get some Mardi Gras beads to string around the handle to make it look super festive.

Toni: What about those shiny beads that ladies like to pull out from down there? We discussed them once at our weekly book club over strong tea. I never thought of using Mardi Gras beads. They come in every shape and size! That may be fun. What do you think?

Ewww! Pull out of where? Never mind. I know where. Toni made me blush, and I rarely blush. Congratulations, Toni. I'm holding my hand over my mouth to stop myself from laughing, and my smile is more of a smirk. Somewhere there is a very Southern woman saying, "Well, I declare, clutch my pearls." Focus, Toni! I need you to stay in the moment with me. You're like a dog playing with a bone. Get to the point, and eat the damn bone. In what women's club do you sit around and talk about shoving strung balls in your cooch? I'd question my club membership. I've seen a few of the other women in your cult, and I have a feeling that your level of kink may be quite different than most. Please don't bullshit me. I know what "strong tea" is because your breath smells of rye whiskey and rapture.

Me: I would stick with the Mardi Gras beads as decoration only. There's no need to buy beads. I have a thousand of them. I'll have a couple of large packages delivered to your room. The adult toy store should have the other beads you're looking for, if you decide to go that route. Here is a list of locations I suggest visiting to get those special items.

Toni: Slap my ass! You know how to treat a woman right. These gifts are going to be the talk of the party. Where have you been all my life? Thank you for the beads. I love having a big package delivered to my room. It makes me feel warm all over.

Seriously, Toni? Too easy.

Me: If you have any other questions, please don't hesitate to ask. Have a nice day, and enjoy our lovely city.

Toni: You got it, darling. I'm going out to make bad decisions. Don't wait up for me!

I'm sad to report that I didn't see Toni again. She never came back to tell me what she bought. The very confusing conversation never got the climax I was hoping for. That's the way it goes in my job, though. Sometimes I get the money shot, and sometimes I get blue balls. I felt used. Toni threw me out of a parked car just like a used condom on homecoming night. I don't know what toys she bought, how she wrapped them up, or what the outcome was. For all I know, she bought elephant-size dildos and doused them with Crystal Hot Sauce. They could have had a sex party in their room, and I'd be none the wiser. It still bothers me that she didn't come back to give me the full scoop. Damn you, Toni! I hope you read this and call me ASAP. I want the details. You'll always be my sexual airhead, and I want more. With that said, I don't have a great ending to this story, and for that I'm sorry. There's something to be said for leaving it up to your dirty mind. A vivid imagination creates a better ending than anything I could write. Enjoy.

DUDE BRO

I love drunk, hung-over fraternity bros. I call them the Dude Bro population. They can be cool as hell or as dumb as a box of rocks. The one thing they all have in common is the way they speak. It's always this guttural, hyper-masculine, stoned way of speaking. It instantly puts you in the most laid-back of moods. They grab their big bull balls, tug with both hands, reach down the front of their pants to unroll their cocks, and then deepen their voices in fear they may come off less bro-ie. My best friend Brett is a Dude Bro. He's the king of the Dude Bro population. He's the most bro-ish, loving, masculine, kick-ass, hot as shit, sexy, caring, compassionate, and fanfartingtastic man you'll ever meet. He hugs me, he tells me he loves me, and never once does he come off as being "gay" or less than the man beast he is. Be like Brett. The world needs more men like Brett. I love you, brother.

Dude Bros can be the worst douchebags or the most interesting people in the hotel. I've talked to the smartest of Dude Bros, who'll one day run the world, and to Dude Bros who can't hold a conversation with a sea slug. I have a dozen stories about Dude Bros, but this one stands out. It's a short conversation, so it'll be a short story. Prepare yourself for the almighty Dude Bro.

I was having a really bad day. I would not have made it through the day if it weren't for meeting Frank. He was hung over from the night before, which is not uncommon here. Frank smelled like a combination of beer, dirt, sex, perfume, and general New Orleans debauchery. Frank's man stank was intoxicating. It rolled over my body like a lover, and I became drunk on it. He was beautiful in that rough kind of way, with thick dark scruff, messed-up floppy black hair, brown eyes, and a hamburger body. My definition of a hamburger body is where an attractive man has a healthy full body with meat on his bones. He works out, but he still loves a good hamburger. He isn't obsessed with the gym, watching every bite he's shoving into his mouth, or drinking massive amounts of protein-enriched shakes. Side note: Protein farts are not attractive or fun. Please keep those smelly farts to yourself. I don't have time for all that juicy mess.

Frank had a green gator on his polo shirt and wore loafers with no socks. Gross. Yes, I look at shoes whether you're a man or a woman. It's not weird; it's me sizing you up to adjust the way I'm going to speak to you. I personally think wearing no socks with any shoes is stepping back into the eighties. Do you want to be the villain from every ski movie ever made? That was a clear sign that Frank was straight and had zero fashion sense. Frank was a catch! Or *was* Frank a catch? Frank opened his mouth, and I wanted to start laughing from the start. The conversation quickly turned into a college comedy.

My job is playing with the English language. I'm admittedly not the best at it, but I love the spoken word as much as the written word. I can turn a phrase into something completely different. One of my guilty pleasures is reading scriptures from the Bible but doing it with an evil inflection. You'd be surprised how different it sounds with something as simple as a change in tone. I ask a lot of questions that wouldn't cross the average person's mind, and I'm not shy about drilling you hard for information. See what I did there? Drilling you hard.

I carefully listen to what you're saying, like a good concierge should. Most people only hear what you're saying, but they aren't listening. Believe me, there's a big difference between the two. I wouldn't be effective in my job unless I understood this basic principle. Here starts the Dude Bro story.

Frank stumbles up to my desk. His nine-inch morning wood is obvious, and he is not hiding it well in athletic shorts. If you're going to charge at me with a sword, then I'm sure as hell going to notice where you're pointing it. He promptly rams his crotch hard into the corner of my desk, flinches, breathes out like he's trying not to vomit, and then stares directly into my eyes. The first impression of someone is always the best. I squint my eyes and shudder. I'm a man. I know how much that hurt. I'm trying not to laugh or throw up from the pain I feel for him.

Me: Good morning, sir. How may I be of assistance?

Frank: Damn, that hurt! I need to watch where I'm slinging my junk.

Me: I hear that. I'm sorry.

Frank: Dude Bro. I feel like hell. Listen, man. I tore it up last night. Where can I get a strong cup of coffee, deodorant, rubbers, and painkillers?

Ouch! You just body-slammed your cock and balls into the corner of my desk. Do you need a hug or a sling? Frank rolled out of bed this morning and felt like utter hell, but he still felt the need to stumble down here for next-day supplies.

I absolutely love that the first thing he thought of was a stimulant, his smell, safe sex, and drugs. He smells perfect to me. He's cute, too. I'm never washing that ball-stained corner of my desk. Thanks, Frank. However, it's New Orleans, and this is not the first time my desk has claimed a victim. It's just the first time a Dude Bro was so vocal about it. There are noticeable scratch marks on his face. He either got into a fight with a cougar or his girlfriend is into rough play. The only way it would've been better is if he'd asked for a shot of whiskey to kill that throbbing pain in his head he must be feeling right now. I've been there. I know that pain. The world is spinning. You promise to God that you'll never do that again until you do it again . . . and again.

Me: There's a small corner store only a block away or a major grocery store twelve blocks away. They're both open now. I'm sure they'd have all the necessary items you're looking for. The grocery store will have better prices and a better selection if you need a certain size. Would you like directions to either of those locations?

Frank: Dude. Bro. I'm not wearing underwear. Is it nippley outside?

I'm disappointed he doesn't catch my obvious flirt. He completely ignores my answers. I'm okay with that, but this is what I'm referring to about hearing and listening. I am listening; he is hearing. This is going to be a fun conversation. I want to know what's racing around in his poor hung-over brain. Let's see what his definition of "nippley" will be. I know the Urban Dictionary version, but as he has made it a point to say he's not wearing underwear, my curiosity is now piqued. Please don't pique my curiosity unless you're ready to deliver a great answer. Frank delivers the answer with excellent Urban Dictionaryesque Dude Bro precision.

Me: Nippley? Do you mean nippy outside?

Frank: Dude. Bro. Nah, I mean nippley. You know, when you go outside, and your nipples hurt. They get rock hard because it's so cold. My girlfriend can explain it better, man, she'll be here in a minute. I love the cold. It makes her titties look huge. I need to be careful in the cold. It gets me in trouble. Especially when I'm not wearing underwear.

Me: It's cool. She doesn't need to explain it to me. I have trouble breathing in the cold. Why do you have to be careful in the cold?

As soon as I say it, I know I shouldn't have. I have opened the magical wardrobe door to Dude Brolandia, and there is no going back for either of us. The lion is wearing tighty-whities, and I can't look away from the bulge. Again, why did he make it a point to say he isn't wearing underwear?

Frank: You know, man. How the cold makes most men shrivel up? You know, man. Not me. I feel that cold wind, and it gives me a raging boner. It makes my cock nippley. Everybody notices it. It's farting huge. And you know, man. I'm like super hard all day. I'm not looking at other women. I can't control it. My girlfriend owns it. You know what I mean, Dude Bro?

Me: I understand what you're saying, and I've never heard of *nippley* being used that way. I learn something new every day. I'm sure she understands. There's nothing wrong with having a strong libido. You just keep doing you, man.

Who are you trying to convince? If you say it's huge, then it's huge. I can see it's huge. Everyone can see it's huge. I didn't think a cock could be nippley, but if you want to take that word away from lady nipples, then who am I to stop you? The Dude Bro complex always revolves around the penis. I don't need the details. Your cold cock is a dangerous pointed weapon? Kudos! I hear you loud and clear. I don't need your girlfriend to explain it to me. I'm here to answer your questions and not analyze your urges or how your penis operates in cold weather. Thanks for the info. I'll place a note in your guest profile. "Dear front desk, guest experiences extreme erections in cold weather. Please assign him a warm room." I'll now be looking at Frank's crotch every time he passes my desk. I'm worried that he may knock down a small child or shatter our glass doors with his giant member running loose in front of him. Frank, thank you for the distraction. It's always a pleasure when I'm warned about impending doom or possibly being impaled by a long sharp instrument.

Frank: It's cool, Dude Bro. I'm going outside to smoke. See how it feels on my junk. Look out for a girl with big titties; that's my girlfriend. Let her know I'm outside, okay?

Me: It'll be my pleasure. Have a nice day, and enjoy our lovely city.

You got me pegged perfectly, dude. I sit in the lobby all day objectifying women with big titties. It's part of my job duties to observe and record all women with big titties and report them to the Big Titty Committee of Greater New Orleans. Do you think I have nothing better to do than be your watchdog? When she comes downstairs, what do I do? It's not like I can walk up to her and say, "You have big titties. Does your boyfriend get a boner in cold weather? If so, you're the woman I'm looking for. He's outside waiting to salute you with his stiff, frozen manhood. Have a great day!" Why do I have a face that invites this type of conversation? I'm not complaining; it makes my life extremely exciting. Frank doesn't come back inside, so I assume he's walking around playing with his wooden fencepost, attempting to impress the local population. Do you know what happens next? You guessed it. His big titty girlfriend walks up to me.

Big Titty: Excuse me, have you seen a guy that looks lost? He was supposed to wait on me. He never listens to me. I don't see him. Is this the only lobby you have?

I see a lot of people who look lost. I'm going to go out on a limb and guess that you're the girlfriend he was talking about. You're not what I imagined. I don't ask her name, and she doesn't volunteer it. I have no better name for her except Big Titty. She is super cool, very hip, big glasses, big hair, pretty smile, and, of course, massive 32DDD breasts. Big Titty has a very small frame. Any size boob would look huge on her, but make no mistake: they are big ole titties. She could have a side job as a professional boob model. For all I know, she could **be** a professional boob model. I don't know her life. She is so ridiculously sticky sweet. I instantly like this girl. It only gets better after she realizes that I've had a semi heart-to-heart with her boyfriend. I'm not shy at using her boyfriend's colorful wording.

Me: I believe you're looking for the man outside. He wanted to check to see if it was "nippley" outside.

Big Titty: Nippley? He's so stupid. Did he brag about having a big cock, too?

Me: He may have mentioned it a few times and a particular cold weather problem he enjoys.

Big Titty: I'm so sorry. His cock is big, but I let him think it's enormous. It's true, though. He can't walk outside in a stiff cold wind without getting an erection. Is that weird?

It's apparent that they've been dating for a long time. Her personality and matter-of-fact way of speaking mirror his. They've picked up each other's mannerisms, but she's more eloquent in the honest way she speaks. Have I met my first Dude Bra? Big Titty has a way of smirking and rolling her eyes after each cuss word that's very endearing. Her doing that small thing makes me forgive her for cussing in public. She didn't need to describe it in detail. I can see it. I'm not blind. She's playing it down so people don't know he's really packing a nine-foot anaconda. I like them both. She is hella cool, and Frank didn't cuss at me or talk down to me. He's like my Brett in every way.

Me: I appreciate the candid honesty. I don't think it's weird, but I'm curious. Is that a win for you or distracting?

Big Titty: I don't mind it. I think it's kinda hot. He likes to talk about my big breasts, too. Did he mention that?

Wow! We became best friends very fast. We didn't even need a first date or drinks. There was no foreplay to build up the tension. We just went fast-forward into a big-titty conversation. Big Titty popped my cherry. She's the first Dude Bra I've ever met, and that's why she made this book. Why can't every woman be a kick-ass Dude Bra?

Me: He may have mentioned that, too, a couple dozen times.

Big Titty: He's lucky he's cute. He puts on this tough-guy act and then cries in every movie we go to. Don't let him fool you. He's harmless. He buries his face in my breasts to hide his eyes in scary movies, too. I'm going to marry him one day.

I don't think that's why he buries his face in your breasts, but you're cute. You're also the best girlfriend in the world. That's true love. Lock him down, girl. You love him so much that you're willing to put his needs and insecurities ahead of your own. You let him believe his manhood is enormous, instead of just "big." You don't judge him, which is one of the most important things not to do. The relationship you see in public is usually not the same in private. It's rare when you can see the truth and a couple has little to hide. I hope Frank knows how lucky he is to have Big Titty in his life. If I swung that way, I would want her as a girlfriend, too.

Me: It sounds like you love each other very much.

Big Titty: We do.

Me: I'm sure he's still outside. There's not much out there to distract him. If you need anything during your stay, please don't hesitate to ask. I'm here all day to assist. By the way, he mentioned he wasn't wearing underwear. There's a mall across the street if you need to buy him a cute pair.

Big Titty: Why would I do that?

Me: Have a nice day, and enjoy our lovely city.

Big Titty: Thank you. Smooches!

Boom! That's how you have a conversation with a Dude Bro and his Big Titty girlfriend. Looking back on the conversation, I wouldn't have changed the outcome in any way. Frank was just being Frank. He may have been hung over, but he was honest. The world may need more Bretts, but it also needs more Franks. The world absolutely needs more Big Titties. She was awesome. I feel bad that I never asked for her real name. I'm the asshole for that. There are times when you listen, times when you hear, and times when you just let the conversation be. For now, I can look back on the experience and smile. How many opportunities does a concierge get to talk about big titties, enormous erections, and love? My life is full . . . Dude Bro.

A NEW ORLEANS
HISTORY LESSON

I believe that children are our future. Cue the cheesy singing and hand-holding. There are two sides to every coin. There is a good side to the young adult coin. These are the young ladies and gentlemen whom I've been so impressed with that not shaking their hands or not engaging in more conversation would be considered a crime. I've taken pictures with them, become friends on social media, and partaken in too many drinks after work. There are times when I never want the conversation to end. I need to remind myself that they're here on vacation and not to visit me.

They will one day be the next presidents of the United States. They will create change for a better future. They will protect the best interests of the American people. They will protect the world for future generations. I'm proud to have met them. I remember them fondly and often wonder what their stories are. What drove them to be the powerful force they are at such a young age? What are their life goals, and how do they plan to achieve them? I want to know their stories, and sometimes I get them.

I met the most amazing young lady the same weekend that this story takes place. We're best of friends now, and I couldn't be prouder of her accomplishments. I love her vibrant personality and her drive to be the best version of herself. She also has a super-cool mom, which is always a big bonus. One day I can see myself with her, sipping wine in Central Park and discussing the state of the world while listening to smooth jazz music. This was the weekend

I met Jillian. Shout-out to you and your mom. You're awesome! Thank you for balancing out my weekend so well. You were the yin to this yang. I dedicate this story to you, but it's not about you. I know you'll get a kick out of it, my beautiful New York City gal. Sip. Sip.

This story is about the other side of the young adult coin, the bad side. These young people are lemmings. They are the people who, if followed, will lead the rest of the world over a high mountain cliff, the bodies falling headlong and smashing onto the jagged rocks below, never to be heard from again. Does this sound brutal? It is.

I had the pleasure of having an annoying conversation with one such young lady. She was a big city girl, but you'd swear she was from the valley of mean dolls. Maybe she was just a valley wannabe? Either way, it was a fun time at the old concierge desk. I say this in jest, of course. Her idea of history made me hurt for our future. Did she go to school? Did she pay attention to her underpaid and overworked teacher? She was mostly irritating and partly fascinating, which doesn't happen too much in my line of work. I immediately knew she couldn't care less about anyone other than herself, which only made my job harder. I'm going to refer to her as Pippa. She was a celebrity socialite party girl in the most stereotypical sense of the word. Her idea of history was not what my idea of history is. I won't spoil the story. Let the pa . . . pa . . . party begin!

Pippa is floating around the lobby, gazing at the lights. She's mumbling to herself and staring at her fingers like they're blurring in and out of focus. Pippa must have ingested a handful of strong mushrooms and didn't share any of them with me. That was her first mistake. I joke. I prefer marijuana over mushrooms. I'm watching her and waiting to see how to handle this mess of a situation unfolding in front of me. Every guest is a different situation, and she's going to be a delightful one.

She darts her eyes at me a few times, and you can see that she's confused as to why there is a middle-aged man sitting at a desk in the middle of a hotel lobby. A concierge is a mystery to the younger Internet generation. They want the instant gratification fix of a cell phone answer, instead of a person-to-person interaction. She begins to approach and then walks away several times. She's either lost in her own thoughts or trying to figure out how to speak.

She's very thin with an almost boyish quality. She's wearing a flowing floral print dress, which gives her an innocent flower child appearance. Her hair is blonde with pink stripes and little kindergarten hair bows. I think she's cute. She makes a phone call, looks up at me, smiles, and then heads straight to my desk. Pippa just used a lifeline, and they told her what I do. She's anything but innocent. She opens her mouth, and it shatters any preconceived notion I might have had. I like Pippa less now.

Pippa: Like, O.M.G., so I totes know what you are now! I had no idea you people still existed. It's like the cutest thing ever in this whole world. Like I want to scream. Soooooo cutes!

Am I a leprechaun? Did I grow a horn and a tail? Did my butt suddenly sprout a fin and I'm squeaking like a deranged Hydra? I'm a human being, not a "you people." I'm the same as you, unless you're an alien. I'm the person who's been waiting for you to approach and say hello. I was thinking of talking to you first, but I decided it was best not to. Thank you for saying repeatedly that I'm cute. It's fake but cute.

Me: Thank you. That's very kind of you to say. How may I assist you today?

Pippa: My dad said you were like this little lobby guy that answers questions. I'm guessing he meant you're like this little booth guy, and you're like a fabo cutes butler or driver or something like that. Soooooooo, like I want to know EVERYTHING. Tell me the history of this city. It's so super dupes like totes cool to be in, like . . . a dirty city. You're the best. Can I literally die here from the heat? I'm totally tripping on how much you can gag me on stuff to eat here. Sooooo . . . the history, it must be so smash me over the head that I don't even know where, like, to begin. My friends are staying here, so lame! I don't care to see them, but they said to drink and take, like, it all in, from gumbolaya to those little powder things. Ugh . . . totes fat kid food! Not that I eat; it's for losers, and I totes prefer a cap. I would love one right now. Sooooo . . . like, make that happen. You know? Like . . . thanks and stuff.

Was there a single question in there that you needed me to answer for you? I need to compliment Pippa on both insulting me and complimenting me in the same diatribe. She did it without ever once cussing or using any directly insulting language. All the information she spit out was always insinuated without her openly saying it. Pippa is a privately tutored smart girl who's using her education in the exact opposite way that it was intended. I don't know where to start. Pippa is all over the place. Do I start with the history of New Orleans? Do you want to know about food to eat? Are you calling the hotel lame or your friends? Did you just order a cappuccino from me, or do you want a suggestion for where you can order one? I'm not making Pippa any sort of coffee drink. That is not in my job description, and that shit ain't happening. I take a deep breath, decide to knock out a few of the basic questions, and then start with city history. Every good story has a backstory, and this city has three hundred years of it.

Me: It's July, so the heat will pretty much be like this for the next two months. Those powder things are called beignets, and they're delicious. I love a good coffee drink, and I know several places for you to get a good one. I'm sorry about your friends, but you'll meet tons of people here. New Orleans has three hundred years of rich history. It's a fascinating city. I'm not a historian, but I can answer most questions. Was there a particular history question you'd like me to answer? We could sit here for a week covering ALL the history of New Orleans.

I receive the "deer in headlights" reaction to my voice. Did I just sprout ten heads again and grow scales? Pippa cocks her head to one side and acts like she is watching a small alien burst out of my chest, singing an Indian spiritual folk song. From the look in her eyes, she has forgotten everything she just asked me. Maybe I'm not cool enough to look her directly in the eyes when I speak to her? I haven't turned into stone yet, so I must be doing something right . . . like totes, so far.

Pippa: What? You. Are. So. Funny. I could just kill you for being so cutes! My dad was right. You. Are. The. Best! Sooooooo like . . . Tell me everything, and I mean totes everything. I want to know it so bad, I could, like, vomit. It's like that time I went to Mexico, and my friend Galisa threw up in her handbag. It was the best . . . like, ever to happen in my life. I felt so bad for her, but not really. She's not my friend anymore because she slept with my bestie who's now gay. Sucks for her. I hate them both. We were on a beach thing tour, and she shouldn't have . . . like drank that much, you know? Ab Fab disgusting and so mortifying . . . for me, of course. I was literally going to puke everywhere, but I, like, had on a new poor shirt. I'd just bought it from this tiny dirty lady on the side of the street. I just felt like I needed to wear it for a day to support her. How cute and boney she was. I wish I was that thin. We bought a little Mexico guy there, too. We got him to drive us, like, around and, like, stuff, you know . . . totes like you, but you're, like, white America cuter. You know? He was not totes cool sweet, and his teeth were totes rotted bad. He told us everything about the scene there. At least, what we could understand from his lame Inglés. It was exactly what we kinda wanted. Can you do what he did? You know, with the little umbrella and then bars. Sooooo, I'm from, like, New York City, and it's, like, the so fab thing to do. Make it happen.

I've never met a New York City girl who talks like you, but okay, let's roll with that. Again, Pippa, I don't know where you want this conversation to go. Pippa's millennial-saturated brain must never slow down, even when she's unconscious. She's processing information in such a small timeframe that it's short-circuiting her motherboard. She's the nicest mean person I've ever met, or does she not know that half the stuff she's saying is cruel? She "bought" a Mexican guy to be their tour guide? No, sweetie, that's not how it works. Rude. The little thin Mexican lady was not on a diet; she's thin and bony because she's poor and hungry. I applaud you for buying a shirt and wearing it for a day, but buy her a meal, too. She would have appreciated it more. Pippa has this fairy-tale look in her eyes, and I have a deep desire to behead her. Her secret weapon is looking cute, but it's not working on me. My tactic will be to act lost in her questions and keep firing back as many answers as I can. When in doubt, redirect the conversation to New Orleans history, and wow the guest with your knowledge of the city. It does not work on Pippa. She's too clueless for that tactic. I am foiled by an animated Valley Girl villain.

Me: I'm sorry, but I'm not sure exactly what I can answer first for you. I can tell you about my favorite city tour companies. I can also make all the arrangements for you. I can set you up with some of the best private walking tours in the city, if you prefer that. I can also cover some basic history and facts about New Orleans if you wish to explore on your own. New Orleans is a three-hundred-year-old city founded by . . .

Pippa: STOP! Like yawn and so totes boring. I don't want to know facts. I want to know everything. You know, like the fun stuff. I want to go home and tell everyone about my so totes awesome time in Nawlins, like you people say it. I want them so jelly of me being here . . . they will die . . . like totes dead in the ground with bugs. Can you make that happen? What a super yawn to learn stuff. It's not N to the Y to the C. When my friends came here last year, they were, like . . . boobs out . . . butt out, they were so trashy that I, like . . . never talked to them again. I'm totes Upper East Side, if you haven't caught on to that. I'm so sorry that you're trapped behind this little desk thingy all day. I will, like, bring you something poor back . . . if that's what you people like and stuff. You're, like, sooooooooooooooooooo cutes.

Pippa is pissing me off. Please, Pippa, cuss at me, so I can call security to haul your ass out of my lobby. Again, I'm not "you people"! Pippa has obviously watched an episode of **Swamp People** and assumes we're all like that down here. She's also kind of morbid. Somewhere muddled in there, it sounded like she wanted me to murder and bury her friends. Can I make their deaths happen? No. That's on you, Pippa. I'm also starting to wonder if Pippa has any friends left to talk to. Everyone she's mentioned she either hates or never talks to anymore. Guess what, Pippa? They probably feel the same way about you. You're rude and shouldn't be allowed in public. You can hide behind your passive-aggressive words all you want, but it doesn't make you any less of a Dziwozona. I'm answering your questions the best I can. I love when people cut me off and say how boring I am. Don't cut people off unless you have a desire to be cut off yourself. This year's blue ribbon for rudest guest goes to Pippa. How is talking to anyone this way acceptable in your glazed-over world? Oh, wait, you don't live in the real world with us normal people. You live in a fairy-tale land of muscular satyrs and glitter-snorting pixies that cater to your every whim. I do want to thank you for that ever-so-sweet offer to fetch me something poor. However, I don't want anything you've touched. Not. One. Damn. Thing.

Me: I'm sorry. I keep missing the mark on answering your questions. What exactly do you want to know more about, and how can I help?

Pippa: Like, duh, but I get it . . . it's a small city full of . . . small people. The only thing that . . . like, you should ever talk about is the bars. That's the only history here that anybody wants to know about. All that, like, other stuff . . . is totes boring. I thought I, like . . . made that, like, perfectly clear many, many times. I want to know, like, everything, meaning everything that's super popular and not, like, lame, meaning the bars and the boys, meaning something you should know about seeing how you are . . . well . . . you. I'm just, like . . . saying.

You dirty ho bag! Did you just imply that I'm gay? That's none of your damn business. How does being gay make me an expert on everything bar related? Being gay doesn't mean I was born with an extra fashion gene gifting me with knowledge on everything from big hair and status-symbol makeup to designer shoes. Do you think I hang out in every club in the French Quarter because I have nothing better to do with my time? How did you guess I travel that big rainbow in the sky? You never made it clear many, many times that you only wanted to know about bars. I feel that I know more about who you hate than what you want to know. You never once mentioned bars, but I guess I should've figured that out from your vomit-filled side comments. I'm so stupid for not piecing that together from your México story. I also hate stereotyping people based on their appearance or the accent in their voice. Pippa is a big-city, nice-talking, backhanded, dirty succubus ho, but I'm not labeling her as one. I'm nice that way. She also just called me small-town stupid, which I'm not. I'm small-town smart and big-city stupid. Get it right. Do you want to do my job? You obviously know better than I do. Pippa is lying about wanting to know all the history of New Orleans. She only wants directions to the local bar scene but doesn't want to sound like a total bar skank about it.

Me: Here's a map. There's Bourbon Street. Walk in that direction.

Pippa: Seeeeeee, that was totes easy. Wasn't it? I'm so going to every bar in New Orleans. Sandra's boyfriend is like totally hot, and I'm going to make him my little slave. If you don't see me before tomorrow, come look for me, K? I'm too adorbs to be left alone. K. Byyyyeeeeee. You. Are. Like. Literally. The. Best. Kisses and stuff. 1 . . . 4 . . . 3!

Me: Thanks. Bless your heart.

I do not say my usual "Have a nice day, and enjoy our lovely city." I dislike her that much. I had to look up 143. It means "I love you" because that's how many numbers match how many letters are in each word. Millennial bullshit rears its ugly head again. Pippa then twirls, floats around the lobby, makes a phone call, giggles, Googles, and walks out the door, leaving a trail of foul-smelling confetti behind her. The flowers wilt as she moves past them, and I swear the sun darkens when she touches the light of day. My mouth fills with blood, as I bite my tongue. I just gave her a map and sent her down the street. It's not exactly what she asked for, but it's what she earned for talking to me like I'm a low-class servant. Who the hell is Sandra? Why in the shit would I care about what presumably slutty things you'll be doing to her boyfriend? Also, for your information, the term *slave* is derogatory and just plain mean. Is she telling me these hateful nuggets about her life because she thinks it makes her look awesome? Guess what? It doesn't. Mean is mean, however sweet you say it. I hope Pippa gets lost in our bar scene, preferably in a gay bathroom where every man with a big thumb thinks she's a dude. I never want to see her again. There will be no search party to find her mean ass if she gets lost. Bye, girl, bye.

My heart aches for the future generation, especially when I meet someone as young as Pippa. I want to wildly shake her. I want to scream at her to make the world a better place, instead of filling it with more hate. I want to cry. Our parents raised us to be a certain way, but we need to be better. Be better than the generation you were born into. Your goal in life should be to raise people up, not tear them down. We're all in this world together, so why not make it the best world we can? Say good morning to a stranger, help someone cross a street, pick up trash that you didn't throw down, hold a door open, help a coworker even if it's not your job, be kind and smile. A smile is easier than a frown. My wish is that one day I meet more people like Jillian and fewer people like Pippa. One day this world will reach a tipping point. In what direction future generations tip is totally up to us. I doubt I'll be around to see the outcome, but I have faith it will tip in the right direction. I have hope that good will overcome the Pippa paradigm.

CASINO CAMMIE

I never win at card games, but I'm good at the game of life. I get the privilege of meeting unique people every single day. They can be hotel guests or just people casually walking by my hotel. I emit a sonic boom that lures in all walks of life from miles away. They're drawn into my seedy world of concierge services from as far as the sidewalk. It's a mystery, but why wouldn't you want to come inside and visit with me? I'm hella funny, I look important, and I've got jokes. The funny thing about being in a very public space is that when I scratch my butt, I have an audience. I'm required to hold question-and-answer seminars after every itch. I joke. Those conversations are only in my head, but wouldn't that be fun?

Let's talk about one of my favorite topics, perception. Perception is a hell of a thing. What you see from a distance is never the same as when it's staring you in the eyes. I've been called a lobby manager, an information specialist, that weird guy at the desk, the person in the know, that dude who can "make things happen," whatever the hell a "conseeeurrgeee" is, a general manager, and my favorite: that man who has answers for everything. I'll take any of those titles. I'm all and none of those. I have a lot crammed in my head, but my best friend is the Internet search bar.

The guest perceives me to be a genius, but I'm far from it. I've been asked your burning question a hundred times before, and I'm regurgitating the information only for you. I'm only human. I make mistakes. I'm not the all-knowing wizard of this land, but I'd never let you know that. Perception happens both ways: from your viewpoint and mine. My perception of people is a long list of varying personalities that can fit into certain categories. They start spinning in my head like a roulette table the moment the guest starts to speak. The ball is bouncing from number to number until it lands on the number I desire. I love when people talk for ten minutes before realizing they're talking to the wrong person at the wrong hotel. I'll hold entire conversations with someone before directing them to the hotel they should be checking in at. I could be sitting inside a glitter-covered glass bubble filled with dancing flowers that smell like premium marijuana, and people will ask if it's the mall. I love when a guest realizes that I'm not the host at that "must eat" restaurant they're looking for. The blank stare they give me will be given back every time with a smirk because they bothered me. It's not that hard to look around and figure out where you are before asking me something so obvious that my dead blind grandmother could've figured it out. I'm not a host at a restaurant podium. What gave it away? Could it be the fact that there is no restaurant in sight or the large Concierge Services sign directly in front of me?

Perception is defined as the ability to see, hear, or become aware of something through the senses. A good concierge has strong perception. The force is strong with me, it is. Most people have it, some people take longer to figure it out, and some people will never be graced by this little gift from God. I listen, take a dramatic pause, and give my answer. Perception has become one of the most powerful tools in my arsenal. It's not 100 percent accurate, however, and this story proves it.

Casino Cammie was not a guest at my hotel. I'm okay with that. You're a guest of New Orleans, so you're a guest of mine. It started out as a very rocky relationship but ended on a good note. We became vacation friends. She would stop in, give me a daily report, have a laugh, and then stumble headfirst into her day. It's one of my favorite exchanges with a rando nonguest. Cammie, I dedicate this story to you.

It's a quiet day at the concierge services desk. I'm twiddling my thumbs, working on reports, reading the daily news, and memorizing the weather for the week. In other words, I'm bored as shit because no one is talking to me. I hate feeling useless. The lobby has an eerie vibe, and it's unmoving. I can hear myself breathing. I'm in a horror movie, hiding under the stairs and waiting for the demon to discover me. My lip quivers, I start to cry, and my eyes are closing. I'm trying very hard not to poop my pants or fall asleep.

I'm staring at an old painting on the far wall in front of me. I've never been able to figure out this piece of artwork. Who thought this was appropriate for a lobby? Is this the first impression we want to give to our guests? "Welcome to our hotel where the artwork is . . . interesting." The women are topless and dancing around a fire with wine glasses in both hands. They all have giant boobs dangling wildly to their knees. They're all rather fetching in that medieval sort of way.

Looking past the main scene, you see something a bit disturbing. Several of the women in the background are chopping off the heads of very brutish-looking men with giant balls and long wangs. The men are sitting down, bound to trees. They are facing forward and appear to be struggling. Their hands are tied behind them to the trees and their legs spread wide open to show off the low-hanging fruit. The men all have very chiseled, athletic bodies with hairy chests. They are the perfection of masculinity. They each have a single sash knotted around the waist but no shirt and no pants. Lying next to them, scattered around the ground like rotting fruit, are severed heads from the poor souls who must have come before them.

Is this Greek? Maybe it's Roman? Why is it hanging in our lobby? It doesn't match any of our décor. Why are they all naked? Is this a sacrifice or a regular hump day Wednesday? Was every man extremely well hung in those days? I can only guess that the women are taking their revenge on the male gender. Maybe it's "bring your husband to work" day, and this is the surprise party. Those poor men. Well done, women. I applaud you. It's not obvious by just a glance, but when you stare at it, the picture is very clear.

I'm creating a world out of the lobby art and slowly forgetting that I'm actually at my job. The world is fading away when I'm rudely ripped out of my fantasy. Help! The demon has found me!

I hear a deep guttural voice, as if Lucifer herself is yelling at me. I know it's not the voice of God, unless God smokes two packs a day and sounds like death. It comes out of nowhere and shakes me out of my dead-eyed glaze. I jump in my seat and pee a little. Don't judge me. Sudden noises have that effect on my delicate little bladder, and it was a tiny amount of pee.

I look over to the side door, and standing there is Casino Cammie. She's tapping her foot with a smirk on her face. I give her a quick look up and down to assess the situation. Perception. She looks like a die-hard, chain-smoking, blackjack-playing, visor-wearing badass from a kick-ass Florida retirement village, if said village were a prison yard with battle-scarred gladiators. Cammie has dark hair, overly tanned snakeskin, nicotine-stained teeth, and a voice deeper than mine. Her hip is cocked out so far that you'd need a detour sign to step around it. It's safe to assume she does serious damage at a casino buffet. That's how I lost a finger. It got bitten off, blocking the Brie cheese. You don't mess around with this chick, or she's gonna kick your ass into the next century.

My first thought is, *Who's this trailer park bag of trash that's yelling at me?* Cammie is holding a pack of cigarettes and two drinks in one hand. She has skills, and Cammie means business. Again, perception is a hell of a thing.

Cammie: Hey! Hey, you squirt! Is this the farting casino?

I've never been called **squirt**. Is that an insult? Should I laugh? Why **squirt**? I'm not a short little skinny dude. I'm muscular and well-built for my frame. **Squirt** does not describe me. Her use of an outdated word is super cute, with just a hint of condemnation added for good measure. The only time you should use the word **squirt** is when you're describing a climactic scene from a porn movie. It should be followed by the "O" face and a round of applause. It's a gross word. It's also one of my favorite words, ranked up there with the word **moist**. I love to use them both when I want someone to cringe a little. Squirt. Squirt. Moist. Moist . . . Moist squirt.

Me: Good morning. The casino is located at the end of the street. You can't miss it.

Cammie: Well, fart this place, you little asshole. Why the shit did I come in here?

You're not wrong. I'm a total asshole, and I was thinking the same thing about you. Why did you come in here? The first thing I want in the afternoon is someone cursing at me. I get plenty of that every other time of the day. You're obviously in the wrong place. How does a hotel lobby look anything like a big casino entrance? Stupid, mean, fart-face lady. Pa . . . tooey! I thought casino trolls knew their way to a blackjack table with no directions needed. I used to live with a casino troll. You could drop that camel toe in the middle of any desert, and she'd know which way to walk on instinct. It's called gamblers' GPS.

I'm about to answer in my sassiest Southern accent when the funniest thing in my life happens. The hurt that befalls Cammie is epic. She doesn't get her head chopped off, but the Greek Gods do listen to my cries. I should have pointed at her and laughed out loud, but I settle for quiet maniacal laughing. Cammie releases the door, and it swings back, hitting her in the face. She tries and fails to stop the door with her other hand, but it's full of precious cargo. Cammie's cigarettes are the first casualty. They slip out of her hand, screaming toward the ground. Men down! Men down! She attempts to catch them with her foot. This only succeeds in splitting the box open. The cigarettes make a run for it and spread over the ground like matchsticks.

Cammie is on one foot now, stumbles, and drops both drinks. One splashes her in the face, soaking the front of her shirt. The other drink dowses out any hopes of smoking those delicious nicotine babies later. They are soaked through and through. The headline reads, "Smokes Tragically Killed by Casino Cammie." I'm a klutz, and this is impressive even by my standards. She then steps backward, trying to regain her balance, and her foot goes out from under her. You got it. She falls right on her big padded ass with a thunderous sound. The building shakes, and the Gods of Olympus gasp from the noise. Muscular, well-hung men break their bonds and push past dancing women, spilling their wine. Justice is served.

Now who's the asshole? Yep! Still me. I laugh so hard, my guts hurt. This is entertainment at its finest. A cruel person would have looked away, but I'm not cruel. I get off my ass and rush to help her. Cammie may have been rude, and she isn't a guest at my hotel, but she's a human being. Fate dealt her a blow. The least I can do is offer my hand. She sounds like a real piece of work, right? However, my perception of this nasty, rude woman is wrong. Why? Keep reading.

Me: Whoa, my Lord. Are you hurt? Let me help you up. Can I get you a towel?

Cammie: You must think I'm a drunken mess of an old lady. Did you see that, squirt?

Me: It was less than graceful. I'm the only one that saw it. It'll be our secret. It could happen to anyone.

Cammie: Don't bullshit me, kid. That was funny as hell. I'm sticky, covered in rum punch, and fell into the middle of the sidewalk. My ass hurts, and all my cancer sticks are ruined. Kick me while I'm down! I deserve it.

I'm kinda digging Cammie's vibe now. Cammie can call me **squirt**. I still think it's a word you only scream out during sex, but I'll allow it. Can I pause a moment and point out she called her cigarettes **cancer sticks**? I love living in the past. Cammie is older, but she's not that old. I want to say, "Your gams look amazing . . . see, you're the cat's pajamas, doll face. You're the bee's knees, sweetheart." I resist the urge to shout out extinct dialogue, but I really, really want to. I also want to kick her since I have permission, but as a good Southern man, I resist. Plus, I am wearing my good shoes, and one must never ruin a good shoe with an ill-advised kick.

Me: I'm not going to lie to you, lady. It was fantastic. Your fall was top ten, and I've seen a drunk bride fall out of a Rolls Royce in full wedding gear. But seriously, are you okay?

Cammie: If this is the worst thing that happens to me on this trip, then I'm farting awesome. Thanks for helping me up. That was very thoughtful of you after I called you a little asshole.

I'm a giant asshole, but let's stick with **squirt**. Where is that rude lady who yelled at me from the street? It's like she isn't the same person anymore. Bipolar much? Was her cussing at me her way of saying hello? I'm guessing a tumble does the body good. Cammie is cool as hell. Beelzebub, she is not. She just made fun of herself, and that's a trait of a wonderful soul. Most people would be upset at the world around them. Cammie is not angry at her clumsiness; she sits there laughing at it. She makes no attempt to cover up her colossal blunder. She owns it, and I love it. Why can't everybody laugh at the silly moments? I'm happy I was a part of it. I grab Cammie's hand and literally pick her off the ground. I dust off her back, as she rubs the rum punch into her shirt. This is the worse wet T-shirt contest I've ever seen. I don't have a problem with boobs. I like boobs. I have burlesque friends, so I get to see them often. However, her boobs look like two underfilled water balloons dangling in mid-air. Cammie doesn't believe in wearing a bra. Good for you! We're both laughing so hard, it takes a few minutes for us to recover. We may be laughing at two totally different things, but all laughter is good for the soul.

Me: Would you like a towel, bandage, ice, or anything else to numb the pain?

Cammie: You're a cheeky little squirt. I have a bagful of stuff that can numb any pain, but thanks. Now, stop fussing over me, I'm okay. Point me to the casino, and I'll get out of your hair.

Is Cammie British? So now I'm not only a squirt, but I'm a cheeky little squirt? Damn it, Cammie. You're making it hard to hate you. Now I'm imagining British squirt porn. It's only watched with afternoon tea and crumpets. The British have very proper etiquette. They're well trained in how to use their pinky fingers. Keep your pinky fingers away from me, readers. Cammie is a master at this game, and she has painkillers of every size and strength. I'm sure she would share if I asked. My new best friend.

Me: I'm glad you're okay.

Cammie: You're very sweet. I guess karma took a chunk out of my big ass, didn't it, squirt?

Me: What?

Cammie: Karma is a bitch. I'm very sorry for the way I treated you.

Karma is a bitch! I'm not shocked that she mentioned karma, I'm shocked she apologized to me. I can count on one hand how many times a guest has uttered those words to any hospitality worker. It's like being asked for spices and dildos. It's like being offered to get your ass eaten at work. It's like I'm a magical, mythical flying unicorn. It's like being hugged by the supermodel of your dreams. It's like meeting a gay man who bitched out a bride. It's like repeatedly being forced to stare at an overripe vagina. It never happens! Oh, wait, those things all happened to me. What the fart! Her first impression of me was a casino doorman she could yell profanities at, with little regard for my feelings. My first impression of her was that she was a rude, mean cow who should die slowly roasting in hell. Isn't it funny how the universe stepped in to change both of our perceptions? People have value. I know that my worth and Cammie's worth are gradually increasing by leaps and bounds.

Me: How about I buy you a drink since you lost two? It's the least I can do. The hotel door did land you a nasty blow. Karma is a lady not to be trifled with. However, Lady New Orleans will embrace you tight and treat you right.

Cammie: I'm not a guest here.

Me: You don't need to be, and I won't tell if you don't. It's on me.

Cammie: I like the way you think.

Me: We're cut from the same cloth, you and me. Please tell the bartender to get you a Pimm's Cup and charge it to me. It's my favorite. Have a nice day, and enjoy our lovely city.

Cammie: Damn nice to meet you, squirt. I'll be back.

*

Cammie became a morning regular at my desk during her vacation. She was visiting New Orleans because she'd earned a certificate for three free nights at the casino. She added on four more nights just for the hell of it. She was making the most out of her New Orleans stay. Isn't life funny? I met Cammie by accident. She walked the wrong way, heard a loud sound, and was drawn into my charming world. She yelled at me because she was frustrated, not because she was rude. Perception is everything. I get it. There have been moments in my life when I yelled at the person and not the situation. Whoever it was probably thought I was an asshole, and, chances are, I was. I try not to be that guy, and I always feel bad afterward.

Cammie would arrive promptly at noon every day to give me the previous day's report. The amount of money she spent at the casino could have bought my house twice over. It amazes me how people can waste their hard-earned money, but is it a waste to them? I'd never spend that much gambling, but it's her life, and she's embracing it with every nickel she drops in a machine. Good for you, Cammie. Different strokes for different folks. Cammie won a hundred dollars, she lost a thousand, she met an old man, she got hit on by a young stud wanting a free ride, she ate a fabulous meal, she ate a crap meal, she fell off a bar stool, she yelled at kids on the street, she slipped on a curb, she found the best po-boy shop in the city, she discovered a love affair with beignets, she slept with a man who stole her streetcar pass, and she drank. She drank way too much. This was her vacation, and she could do whatever the hell she wanted to do.

I did laugh a little every time she mentioned how often she fell or tripped. Her experience in falling out of my lobby door was nothing new to her. It was just a normal day in the Cammieverse. Cammie wakes up, she drinks, she falls, and she repeats. I hope she has great health insurance. We got to know each other so well during her non-stay at my hotel that Cammie let me in on a little secret. The concierge at her property "sucked ass." I laughed out loud. I guess not every concierge is comfortable laughing at a guest like I am. The reason she kept coming to my hotel was because she felt we were friends, and so did I. She loved my suggestions, and she felt comfortable talking to me. She also totally loved my name. Well, duh, it's an awesome name.

We keep up with each other, and she calls my desk now and then just to check in. I'm happy to report that she'll be bringing friends back to stay at my hotel. She promised to fall out the door at least once and will encourage her friends to do the same. I told her it was a requirement for staying here. I want more people like Cammie to come back to New Orleans. I truly want guests to love their time here, whether they stay with me or not. You can fall, get drunk, laugh at me, or laugh at yourself. The only thing I ask is that you always call me *squirt* and provide me with hours of entertainment.

DoodleMaBob by Joshua Carpenter, *My No Place Like Home*

CHAPTER FOUR

MY LIFE TODAY

This is my world through the eyes of Ren. The party never ends, but it's time for me to clock out and wrap this up. The daily dialogue continues at my desk, and I'm taking notes for the next book. Did you skip the first two chapters? Skip this one, too. I won't be offended. This chapter is the wrap-up, and it's all about me. I'm super lame. There're no funny guest stories of high jinx and mayhem in this chapter. There're no flaming bag of dicks references, except for this one, and no funny quips of frustration. I'm about as ordinary as they come. I get up in the morning, brush my teeth, drink coffee, feed my dogs, scratch my ass, jump into my suit, and pick out my favorite bow tie.

Every day is a new adventure. I get through the long day thinking that every day is Christmas. I get to unwrap a shiny new present every morning at work. I never know if I'll get a golden goose or a giant purple turd. The guest is the wrapping paper, and the conversations are the reward. I would love to say that I remember every interaction I've had, but I don't. There are some that stand out and honestly a few that I've completely forgotten. The ones that really stand out made this book, and the rest, I'm keeping in my back pocket for later. If you didn't see your story here yet, wait for it.

I stroll into work half asleep with a goofy look on my face, craving another cup of coffee. I say a sleepy hello to all my coworkers and try not to yawn. I start typing away at my workstation, hitting buttons with the speed of a jackrabbit. You don't know what I'm doing, and half the time neither do I. The harder I hit the keys, the more important I look. Fooled you, didn't I?

Every day I have the pleasure of listening to these top billboard hits: "Arrange this! Schedule that! I don't understand why you can't be in two places at once. Fix it! Make it work! I thought you were Superman. You're not very super. Why can't you magically pull a rabbit out of your butt for my daughter's birthday? It's my birthday, and no one in the world has a birthday today but me. My wife and I do this cool thing that no other couple does, called an 'anniversary.' The world should celebrate the fact that we haven't killed each other yet. This is my wife, and we're on a honeymoon because no one in history has ever thought of celebrating this day. We're on vacation, and we expect everything to be free because we spent our last two pennies on the plane ticket here. You're awesome. You're amazing. How do you remember so much history of New Orleans? You're so cute. I mean, totes cute. Can you go with us and be our super-duper tour guide? We don't want to pay you, though. Bro, that's so dope. Can you tell me what's growing between my toes?" Ewwww!

I say yes to most everything, with an occasional head nod thrown in for good measure. I smile big, even when I don't want to. I should wear a metal jingle bell because I'm constantly getting up and running around. I don't like to stay in one place for very long, although I'm required to be at this desk 99 percent of the day. Watch me whip, watch me move, watch me sashay away. I dance, I sing, and I type up our conversations. I'm one day closer to retirement . . . or death? Why be still when the world moves so fast around us? I always want to be in motion. The day I sit still will be the day I miss my moment. The older I get, the more I realize that my moments are passing me by. How depressing is that to think about? Sorry.

Lately, my life has revolved around hospitality industry gossip. It's a fun game. There are only so many guest stories to go around. I love when vendors sit next to me and gossip. You don't say? An award-winning celebrity chef is sleeping with a member of the kitchen staff. Scandalous! The partner doesn't care and is banging half the wait staff? Yes! It's an open secret? Then hell yes! Get your groove on. A corrupt tour company had a hostile takeover and is now being run by a titan in the industry? You don't say. Tell me more. He's paying top dollar and poaching the best tour guides in the city? Girl, I'm there. A tour company let go of their most seasoned, well-respected public relations manager? How dare they! She wants to open her own tour company. You better believe I'll be kissing her ass on both cheeks. Good thing I'm one of her best friends. Someone was caught sleeping with his best friend's wife! What happens in the sheets stays with me, my peeps. There's a new tour guide in town. His nickname is Donkey Dong! You better believe I'm gonna be all eyes downtown. He is one fine, blue-eyed representative. Thank you, bro! That fancy five-star restaurant failed its health inspection because they found rat droppings in the cooler! That's nasty, and they'll never get my business again. Trust me on that one.

Gossip. There's nothing better than gossip, and I get to hear it all. I'll smile, listen, and then pick up the phone. Gossip is power, and it generates buzz. Concierges are all about the buzz. A concierge has influence on a business whether you believe that or not. A creative description or suggestion from a concierge can mean the difference between selling out a restaurant or the manager sitting alone.

I've said it a thousand times. You can't get human emotions from a computer, but you can from a hotel-employed concierge. A concierge is better than any search engine and always will be. Instead of denying the gossip, run into it headfirst. Do you know what repairs the damage of gossip? A hug. A hug means more to me than any catty gossip. It can repair most damage, followed by an honest explanation. If the world ran on hugs and honesty, it would be a better place. Granted, a hug doesn't tip or pay my bills, but you'll have my respect, and I'll feel loved.

A story is only as good as the person telling it. Every good story has a beginning, a middle, and an end. My wonderful life is similar, hopefully with the end coming decades from now. What happened after my conception as a concierge? It's playing out day by day, with each episode more interesting than the next. Time marches on with very long days, hilarious hours, and every minute that seems to never end. This crazy thing called life.

Currently, I live with my amazing, wonderful boyfriend Joshua. He's an Oscar-winning actor whom Hollywood moguls fight over daily—at least, that's how I see him. We're boyfriends, partners in crime, fur daddies, explorers, lovers, and, most important, best friends. It could be the worst day of my life, and he makes everything better when he walks in the door. There are days I want to slap the shit out of his silly ass, but that's part of the gig. I love him with all my heart.

My boyfriend told me to "manifest my destiny." What kind of make-believe bullshit is that? I didn't understand what that meant, at first. I've worked hard and struggled for every inch of ground I earned. Was I manifesting my destiny but didn't know it? Yes, I had been my whole life, but it took him saying it for me to see it. I wanted to become a better person, so I became a person I could be proud of. I wanted to change my dull retail occupation, so I became a hospitality professional. I discovered that I love conversing with people from around the world, and I'm good at it. I wanted to buy a new car, buy a new house, grow a vegetable garden, buy the lot next door, adopt the perfect dogs, meet my endgame boyfriend, and write a book. I did it all. I manifested my destiny. The goals in my life have always been attainable because they're achievable for anyone who believes in him- or herself. Am I finished manifesting my destiny? Hell, no!

My dream is to one day be a father. I want to throw a ball and my son will catch it. When he falls off his bike and starts crying, I want him to know that I'll always be there to pick him up. I want to bang loudly on the bathroom door, bust him for smoking, see him fall in love with the girl or the boy next door, and watch him grow into the man I know he can be.

My son will be raised in the cutest New Orleans bed-and-breakfast. My boyfriend will never change a diaper, but he will change the sheets. I can picture it vividly. The B&B will have a main house for us to reside in, with a large front room to entertain our small group of guests. There will be a center courtyard for garden parties, connecting four different-colored cottages. Each cottage will have a unique name to reflect the diversity and love of New Orleans. There will also be a small theater, just for the hell of it. The nightly shows will feature local plays and will premiere new artists, burlesque performers, and all the storytellers I can pack into it.

It will happen, but until then, it's nice when you find someone you can just fart next to and laugh. He also endures endless farts from our two giant dogs: Jasper and Nami. Life is stress free with only blissful, silent, deadly, stinky, creeper farts. What's the secret to a happy life? Have room spray in every room. Relationships are work, but the best ones shouldn't feel like work. Relationships with guests are very similar. I build them every day. I love to breathe in some, and others I spray away. Each guest is different, and each relationship has a different reward.

Many people have asked me, "Why title your book *Creating a Concierge*?" There is no correct answer. Call it creation, evolution, or chance, but ultimately it's what felt right. My stories, conversations, and choices brought me to this point in my life. I'm the product of how I was raised by my parents, the way I was treated while growing up, and the interactions I've had with the people in my life. These interactions include all the times I was called worthless, unlovable, untalented, small, ugly, poor, useless, forgettable, and stupid and was treated as less than the amazing person I am. They also encompass all the times I felt compassion from another and was encouraged, loved, praised, laughed with, smiled at, genuinely hugged, and reminded of my value. They even include all the times I was pushed to be more than just a bartender, a server, a retail worker, a front desk agent, a writer, a whore, an asshole, or the thousand other labels I've been saddled with over time. I'm not "just" a single label; I'm all of them. I said this at the beginning of the book, and it still holds true at the end of the book: I'm a good person. At the end of the day, the only label that matters is the one you call yourself. The spark of life is real, and you only need to open your eyes to see it.

It has been my pleasure to write this book. I hope it made you laugh, cry, love, and smile. I do have one request. The next time you travel to a city, whether it's New Orleans or some other far-away land, remember these stories. Treat the staff with respect. There will be broken air conditioners, food not cooked perfectly, a bag lost, an item you left behind, a wallet stolen, a car brought around late, a bad suggestion from a concierge, a horrible tour, bad weather, unexpected fees, bad directions, bad bartenders, a room not cleaned, a toilet broken, a hair dryer missing, a check-in time that is not met, and a thousand other shitty things that will ruin your vacation.

Please, remember to breathe and be kind. It's not the end of the world. Your firstborn child was not sacrificed to the hotel overlord of Tartarus. Calm down. You'll survive the traumatic event that just befell you. The hotel staff is working hard to make your stay great, but we do screw shit up. Being on this side of the desk is not as easy as it looks. The overall theme I'm trying to drill into your thick skull is simple. Don't be a jerk, or you'll find yourself in the pages of a trashy bargain-bin concierge book. Hint. It's this one.

Thank you. Have a nice day, and enjoy our lovely city. ☺

THE END

DoodleMaBob by Jeff Strahan Jr., *Jasper and Nami*

A LITTLE SOMETHING EXTRA

My favorite friends are listed below as a little extra happy. Enjoy!

1. **Karma:** Destiny or fate in future existences. My girlfriend if I swung that way.
2. **Choice:** An act of selecting a decision when faced with two or more possibilities.
3. **Asshole:** A person's anus—or, me on a bad day . . . or a good day.
4. **Squirt:** To be ejected from a small opening in a thin, fast stream or jet—or, a person perceived to be insignificant, impudent, or presumptuous. British porn.
5. **Gossip:** Casual or unconstrained conversation or reports about other people, typically involving details that are not confirmed as being true. My favorite thing ever!
6. **Hyperbole:** Exaggerated statements or claims not meant to be taken literally.
7. **Rhetoric:** The art of effective or persuasive speaking or writing, especially the use of figures of speech and other compositional techniques. Words I'm bad at using.
8. **Reality:** The world or the state of things as they actually exist, as opposed to an idealistic or notional idea of them. The world in which Ren rarely lives in.

9. **Perception:** The ability to see, hear, or become aware of something through the senses.

10. **Exposition:** A comprehensive description and explanation of an idea or a theory.

11. **Persuasive:** Good at persuading someone to do or believe something through reasoning or the use of temptation . . . or being a smartass . . . or creating a concierge.

12. **Descriptive:** Denoting or relating to an approach to language analysis that describes accents, forms, structures, my balls, and usage without making value judgments.

13. **Narrative:** A spoken or written account of connected events; a story . . . or my life.

14. **Hypermasculinity:** A psychological term for the exaggeration of male stereotypical behavior, such as an emphasis on physical strength, aggression, and sexuality. Dude Bro.

15. **Integrity:** The quality of being honest and having strong moral principles, moral uprightness; the state of being whole and undivided; in other words—don't be a liar.

16. **Respect:** A feeling of deep admiration for someone or something elicited by his or her abilities, qualities, or achievements, the way the world should universally be.

17. **Love:** An intense feeling of deep affection, a great interest, and pleasure in something, a person, or a thing that one loves—or, THE WAY YOU SHOULD TREAT EVERYONE!

DOODLEMABOB GALLERY

DoodleMaBob by Joshua Carpenter, *Dude Bro*

DoodleMaBob by Joshua Carpenter, *Dinner for Italians*

DoodleMaBob by Gustave N. von Bodungen, *A Pigeon and His Lady*

DoodleMaBob by Gustave N. von Bodungen, *Lady V*

DoodleMaBob by Sarah Ruhland, *A New Orleans History Lesson*

DoodleMaBob by Sarah Ruhland, *Alternate Conversations*

DoodleMaBob by Thomas Foster, *Lady Beverly of Awesomeshire*

DoodleMaBob by Ashlee Polson, *A Guest Travels*

ABOUT THE AUTHOR

Ren French is a New Orleans–based playwright, actor, and award-winning hotel concierge. His wildly successful old-time radio series, *The Clifton Monroe Chronicles*, has been performed on stages throughout New Orleans. His other series include *Saints and Sisters—Nuns with Guns in Old New Orleans*, *The Chip Parker Journals*, and *A Crescent City Christmas*. In addition, Ren has also written short stories, told many tall tales, and performed as a burlesque member of *Picolla Tushy Presents: The Bluestockings*.

Ren has bitten his tongue for more than thirty years in guest services and now shares his experiences with you, the reader. Enjoy outlandish personalities, dumb guest questions, crazy conversations, and glimpses of his life leading up to and through the lens of a concierge. The internal dialogue in Ren's mind, as opposed to what Ren says to the guest, is a fun journey through the fantastical world of *The Rensverse*.

Ren currently lives in New Orleans with his family: actor Joshua Carpenter and their two amazing and gassy fur-kids, Jasper Pendragon and Namaste Panini.